NORTH CLYDE ESTUARY

AN ILLUSTRATED ARCHITECTURAL GUIDE

HAILING FROM INVERNESS, I was taken by surprise quite recently when I read through the guide to the Moray Firth area. Despite many forced explorations of the area in my childhood, I was quite unaware of the visual interest to which I had obviously grown over familiar.

In the same manner, I expect this guide may surprise many of those who live and travel within the North Clyde Estuary. The contrast between the bustle of a commercial centre and the sheer tranquillity and beauty of our west coast, for example, is almost unrivalled in such proximity. This accessibility tempts the voyager to dart through and beyond a rich and varied piece of our country which offers great beauty to those willing to slow down and look.

Frank A Walker and Fiona J Sinclair are to be congratulated for their fine blend of history, geography and architecture as is Anne Dick for the visual support. They give us a guide guaranteed to increase our awareness of an area often overlooked.

Eddie Riach

E C RIACH
PRESIDENT
Glasgow Institute of Architects

© *Authors: Frank Arneil Walker and Fiona J Sinclair*
Series editor: Charles McKean
Series consultant: David Walker
Cover design: Dorothy Steedman
Editorial consultant: Duncan McAra

Royal Incorporation of Architects in Scotland
ISBN 1873190 07 7
First published 1992

Cover illustration:
Archibald McMillan Shipyard, Dumbarton painted by Samuel Bough
(courtesy of National Maritime Museum, London)

Typesetting, page make-up and picture scans:
Almond Design, Edinburgh
Printed by Pillans & Wilson, Edinburgh

A

Along the entire stretch of the northern shores of the Firth of Clyde no physical feature arrests the eye more than the craggy basalt protuberance of Dumbarton Rock. As Ailsa Craig bursts abruptly from the waters of the Firth far to the south so the great Rock thrusts itself out of the flat coastal landscape where the Leven winds slowly into the Clyde. From earliest times until the 18th century, its natural fortress-like form and its strategic position made it the key to the region. Who held the Rock commanded not only the east/west route to the Firth and beyond but the way north into the heart of Scotland.

Hemmed in by the Kilpatrick Hills, a narrow riverside plain extends from Glasgow across the Leven Valley and up into Gareloch. To the west, beyond this thin riparian crescent, lie Loch Long, Cowal and the Isle of Bute, the mountainous sea-girt margins of Argyll. North, by the Leven, lies Loch Lomond, over 20 miles of it penetrating through Glen Falloch to the Highlands, its eastern shore opening up a gentler approach through Strathendrick to Stirling.

Established in post-Roman days as the capital of the ancient British kingdom of Strathclyde, Dumbarton's regional importance as a base from which to control the west became a frequent cause of contention and conflict in the emergence of Scotland as a medieval nation state. From the creation of their fiefdom in the 12th century until its virtual dissolution at the end of the 17th, the Earls of Lennox – the name may be a corruption of Levenax or Levenach, *the field of Leven*, and applied more or less to the area of latter-day Dunbartonshire – were repeatedly in dispute with the Crown.

Despite the recurring struggles to possess its castle, the town of Dumbarton, which had received the important trading privileges of a royal burgh in 1222, prospered slowly if not spectacularly, first as a market and port but later – more than half a millennium later – as a centre of manufacturing and industry. Developing a little to the north of the castle rock, the curve of its medieval main street ran *concentric with and near the course of the Leven*, both street and river to a chance degree reflecting the crescent curve of Dunbartonshire's own coastline. It was this relationship of town to firth which meant most to Dumbarton in its early growth.

Opposite: *The Hill House, Helensburgh (photo Anne Dick)*

Below *Dumbarton Rock and the River Leven*. Bottom *Dumbarton Castle*

Ralston Photography

SDD

Leven shipyard, Dumbarton c.1880

Dumbarton District Libraries

Although in 1658 it lost the opportunity to serve as Glasgow's deep-water port, Dumbarton managed to retain its right to levy customs dues on all vessels sailing between the River Kelvin in the east and the head of Loch Long to the west – but only until 1700 when it sold out to Glasgow. This loss, coupled with the subsequent deepening of the Clyde, meant that the town had to surrender all hopes it might have had of attaining mercantile pre-eminence on the river. Nonetheless, the late 18th century saw new industries develop. A major glass and chemical factory was built, its three giant cones dominating the skyline until their demolition in 1850, while along the upper reaches of the Leven bleaching and printing works were creating a new landscape of stone and brick as red as the Turkey red dyes for which Renton, Bonhill, Alexandria and Jamestown became famous.

From the 1830s shipbuilding began to emerge as Dumbarton's principal industry, the name Denny becoming world-renowned. River improvements on the Leven benefited the yards and an extensive range of industries such as foundries, engine and boiler works, rope and sailmakers, etc. grew up in support. As a harbour Dumbarton may not have flourished as did Greenock or Glasgow itself but in building ships the town proved every bit as successful and notable.

The Leven marks a significant divide not just in the topography of the north bank of the Clyde but in its economic life. To the east is that same industrial legacy which shaped the Victorian prosperity of Dumbarton and the Vale: textiles in Milton and Duntocher, shipbuilding and marine engineering in Clydebank. But to the west everything seems devoted more to leisure than to work.

Cardross is leafy and rural. Helensburgh, a gridded garden suburb looking south across the Firth, is already a holiday town of esplanades, cafés and yachts. Further on where the yachts sail, are the steep-sided lochs of a wilder more romantic scene. Here, where almost every settlement once had its pier (most no longer do) development came by boat – the puffing paddle-steamer bringing the shipping magnates and ironmasters, lawyers and stockbrokers, who built their castle retreats and villas west from Shandon to Cove, along Cowal shore from Blairmore to Toward, and on Bute from Port Bannatyne to Ascog. Later came the riveters and boilermakers, fitters and turners, plumbers and joiners streaming *doon the watter* from the shipyards for their Fair week or fortnight in Dunoon or Rothesay to live in boarding houses or rented tenement flats and laugh and sing in the Pavilion or Winter Garden.

British silk dyeing factory, Balloch, c.1830

But here there were older settlements, too: cottages clustered around ferry point or sheltered inlet; castles at Innellan and Toward, with one of Scotland's finest and oldest at Rothesay; great aristocratic houses such as Rosneath and Mount Stuart; and ancient churches such as the ruined tower-house rump of Kilmun Kirk and the hauntingly spiritual stones that still stand in the remote glade of St Blane's at the far south end of Bute. And all of this so distant from the clangour of the yards in Clydebank or Dumbarton – and yet so near.

Left *Dunoon Castle.* Below *The Old Smiddy, Rosneath*

The Gareloch, engraving c.1830

Organisation of this Guide

This Guide begins upriver at Clydebank and moves west to Dumbarton. From this historic T-junction on the north bank of the Clyde, the route north is followed, first through the Vale of Leven to Loch Lomond – *romantic beyond imagination*, Smollett called it – north east into Strathendrick, and then north along the Loch to Inverarnan. Returning to Dumbarton, the Guide moves west to Helensburgh, on around Gare Loch and up Loch Long to Arrochar.

Argyll is then explored, but only its eastern shoreline below the hills of Cowal from Ardentinny in the north to Toward and Loch Striven in the south. Finally, comes Bute, softest and greenest of the west coast islands.

Text Arrangement

Entries follow the format of name (or street number), address, date and architect. Descriptions of streets and lesser buildings have been contained within paragraphs. Illustrations have been included of buildings now demolished. The dates given are those of the completion of the buildings (if known) or design. The accompanying margin text deals with historical aspects of the area.

Right of Access

Many of the buildings described in this Guide are either open to the public or are visible from the road. Some, however, are not so readily seen while many are privately owned and readers are asked to respect the occupiers' privacy.

Maps

The maps were prepared by Fiona Sinclair and Frank Walker with thanks to the M V Nicolson series. Principal locations are named on the end map; there are street maps of the main towns. The reference numbers relate to numbers in the text and not to page numbers.

Sponsors

This Guide would not have been possible without the support of Dunbartonshire Enterprise, Argyll and the Islands Enterprise, Dumbarton District Council, Clydebank District Council, John Brown Engineering and The Helensburgh & District Civic Society, whose generous financial assistance has helped to lower the cover price of the book.

Clydebank District Libraries

CLYDEBANK

Shipbuilding was started here by James and George Thomson who, moving downriver from Govan in 1871, bought the West Barns o' Clyde land opposite the debouch of the Black Cart Water and immediately west of the old Junction Canal that linked the Clyde to the Forth & Clyde waterway at Whitecrook. In 1899 they sold out to the Sheffield steelmakers, John Brown and Co., whose ships – *Lusitania*, *Aquitania* and the three Queens amongst them – established *Clyde-built* fame world-wide.

From the Glasgow boundary at Yoker to Dalmuir in the west, the evidence of a prosperous past remains: exhausted docks and shipyards, dereliction that renewal has scarcely healed, the sad nostalgia of the town's motto *Labore et Scientia* cut in the stonework of the municipal buildings. **Rothesay Dock**, 1900-7, a mile of quayside around 20 acres of water, is all but deserted. The vast expanse of railway track that once handled shipments of coal and ore has vanished. There are no trainloads of workers disgorging from

1 **Clydebank Riverside Station**, 1896; J J Burnet's red brick and sandstone building, with its low bartizaned corner entrance hall, piended dormers and chimneyed ridge, looks redundantly decorative in bleak surroundings.

North of Dumbarton Road, across the Forth & Clyde Canal, the town's other major employer, the Singer Sewing Machine Co., located the **Singer Works**, 1882-5, Robert McAlpine, a huge spread of red brick factories, from which rose a domed tower with *the largest clock in Europe*, demolished in 1980 to make

'Queen Elizabeth' and Clydebank East

Bill Wright, who grew up in wartime Clydebank, remembers the awesome nights of the blitz: *Men flew across half of Europe to drop bombs on a short stretch of a ribbon of river where essential shipyards were packed end-to-end on both sides of the bank. The workers lived with their families in houses one on top of the other and formed the outside edge of the ribbon. Nothing more convenient than living near your work. Night visitors were seeking industrial targets and finding them, but when you lived near your work ...*

Riverside Station

Dick

7

Black Arrow building

2 way for **Clydebank Business Park**, a development of new low-scale factories in a now almost rural landscape. Along **North** and **South Avenues** black glass and curved silver cladding shine with optimism. The **Black Arrow** building, 1985, Carl Fisher Sibbald & Partners, has been designed for transverse expansion with an exposed framework of castellated steel sections. Less high-tech are the oblique rustic brick forms, wide eaves and balconies of the **Radio Clyde** building, 1983-4, William Nimmo & Partners.

Thomsons' Yard and Singer's Works brought Clydebank into existence; so that when the town won burgh status in 1886, Thomsonstown and Singerstown were canvassed as possible names. The more innocuously topographical *Clydebank*, which was also the name of the Thomsons' old Govan Yard, stuck – although *Tamsons' Toon* continued to be used to describe the tenements built close to the shipyards.

Municipal Buildings

3 **Municipal Buildings**, Dumbarton Road, 1900-2, James Miller
Miller's design reacts to its corner site by raising a high plain tower to hinge the composition and mark the focus of the town's administration. The *Angel* figure, once above the tower, now in the foyer after the storms of 1968, came from the 1901 Glasgow Exhibition. The façade is agitated by heavy quoining but dignified by a frontispiece of coupled columns and some fine carving. On Hall Street a chunky first-floor pilastrade links to the former **Police Buildings**, a recessed gabled front whose thermal window is flanked by twin towers with wide eaves and depressed Palladian windows. Opposite were the tenemented **Fire Station** and gabled **Public Baths**, both by Miller, the latter providing steam for plenum heating which served all four buildings until 1979.

4 **Public Library**, 1912-13, A McInnes Gardner
From fifteen competition entries Gardner was
named winner by the adjudicators, amongst
whom was James Miller, architect of the town's
Municipal Buildings – and Gardner's previous
employer. The choice was good: a powerfully
horizontal façade of giant Ionic columns with a
decided hint of French historicism.

Public Library

Some *Tamsons' Toon* tenement townscape has
been saved. East of the Municipal Buildings to
the art deco corner of **Woolworths**, 1938-9,
Wallace Street, the rehabilitated ranges of
Centenary Court, 1986, maintain street-line
containment. So do **71-113 Dumbarton Road**
running west from the Library. At **421-481**,
1906, continuity is re-established in higher,
later, flats with canted bays (note the
5 dreadnought carved on the corner at second
floor). At **491-523**, 1986 – busy polychromy,
bracketed eaves and pert little porches –
Scottish Special Housing Association (SSHA)
architects have sacrificed scale and urbanity to
fussy modishness. Intermittent tenements and
a one-off crow-step gabled façade at **627**
reaffirm dignity, while at **709-781 Dumbarton
Road** and in **French Street, Castle Street**
and **Castle Square**, *c.*1914, red sandstone
ranges, with square and saltire motifs cut in
canted bays, restore some enclosure.

On the north side of the road the mirror
cracks and everything has disintegrated into
an indecisive collage of open space and
pusillanimous *new-build*. **Kizil Mansions**,
1913, at **103 Glasgow Road**, sports a domed
6 corner and *wally* close, while **Whitecrook
Street**, *c.*1900, has kept a fine tenement range
with front stairs and unusual segmentally
hooded close entries. At **Nairn Place**, 1981,
housing by SSHA architects is full of interest
and quality in detail, but by no means urban
enough in scale. Only in Dalmuir do the
tenements return: from **Dunn Street** to **Scott
Street** four sandstone canyons, their
relationship with Dumbarton Road excised
by the blitz, dwarf more well-intentioned but
scarcely urban polychromatic brick infill.

More isolated are those church buildings
which have somehow survived along the length
of the A814: **Hamilton Memorial Church**,
1884, neo-Norman with a tall spire, slim in
form but hefty in detail; **Holy Redeemer's
Church**, 1902, P P Pugin, its façade gable
lanceted and buttressed; **St Columba's**

Below *Carved dreadnought,
Dumbarton Road*. Bottom
Whitecrook Street

Episcopal Church, 1896-7, low and cruciform with a Star of David window in the east; and 7 the former **Union Church**, 1893-4, J B Wilson, short in the nave, but richly Perpendicular in its twin-towered gable.

Attempts to restore social focus to Clydebank have been tied to the line of **Kilbowie Road** which links the old riverside burgh across a swathe of canal, railway and industry to the upper town of **Radnor Park** and **Boquhanran**. It begins in the rump of **Alexander Street**, c.1885, where some three-storey shops and tenements, 1887, 1895, connect with Glasgow Road. These properties were built by the once-powerful Clydebank Co-operative Society which 8 also erected the **Central Warehouse**, 1914-17, Stewart & Paterson, a high red sandstone screen which swings around the curved corner with Chalmers Street.

9 **Clyde Shopping Centre**, 1978-83, Hugh Martin & Partners
Alexander Street continues to **Sylvania Way South**. First, the space is spanned by a castellated beam structure; next comes a glazed barrel vault (now the ubiquitous hallmark of shopping malls); and then a space-deck thrown over a ramped bridge which crosses the old canal. Close by, in a landscaped square, sits a cast-iron **bandstand**, 1907, moved here from Whitecrook Park. The route turns, continues, and turns again. Franconia Square opens but is cluttered with sculpture, trees, plants, seats and lights. Connection north continues while another glazed mall in red tubular steel runs back east to more supermarket shopping. Brash and bright, this is the nearest Clydebank comes to a town centre.

District Council Offices, 1979, Baxter, Clark & Paul
Variations – but not many – on a pre-cast concrete panel system also used by the architects for the offices of John Brown Engineering Ltd.

Upper Clydebank is almost wholly residential. After the destruction of the tenemented town during two devastating night raids by the Luftwaffe, a massive programme of re-housing was undertaken in low-, medium- and high-rise blocks; more than half the housing stock being in four-in-a-block cottages. The town seems to have spread endlessly in confusing mazes of contoured avenues and drives and despite all the good intentions,

Below *Central Warehouse.*
Bottom *Clyde Shopping Centre*

Clydebank District Libraries

The devastation of the blitz

On the nights of 13-14 March 1941 a devastating blitz rained down on the shipyards and munitions factories of Clydebank. *Young children were wakened in the middle of the night and forced into daytime clothes over the top of pyjamas and nightgowns by anxious parents. A distinctive, sleep-shattering wailing filled the air ...* By morning over 4000 houses had been totally destroyed; of a stock of 12,000 houses only eight were undamaged. The scale of destruction was immense and the catastrophe for the Bankies all but final, *their homes, bodies, family groups, traditions, minds ripped apart.* Half a century on, the recovery is still underway.

evident in the socialist commitment of names such as Attlee Avenue, Cripps Avenue, Dalton Avenue, etc., and the sheer scale of the endeavour, a sense of blighted optimism is inescapable. Only the leafiness of some earlier streets, hedge-lined or tree-planted, saves the day. Along **Duntocher Road** towards **Dalmuir Park** some older villas, *c.*1875, have survived war and renewal.

10 **Melbourne House**, Regent Street, 1890
Symmetrical, pavilion-roofed, with square bays carrying a hefty entablature over an Egyptian-columned veranda, this robust mansion must surely be the work of Alexander Thomson's last partner, Robert Turnbull.

Montrose Street, 1891, **Clarence Street** and **Cambridge Avenue** form a gridded enclave of red sandstone terraces, gabled, bayed and dormered, with a more recent tightly designed flat-roofed row inserted in red brick along the south side of Cambridge Avenue, 1966. At **Bannerman Place**, 1980, variation of block plan, ridge height and roughcast colour has been used to good effect. Even high-rise can work occasionally: five 13-storey towers, spaced generously along **Kirkoswald Drive**, 1964-5, succeed by virtue of their location.

Clydebank Technical College, 1965, 1969, 1970, T Cordiner & Partners
Concrete-framed boxes for learning in, bleakly packaged in brick and mosaic panels. Nearby is **Kilbowie St Andrew's Church**, 1902-4, tower 1933, formerly St John's-on-the-Hill, a low cruciform red sandstone kirk in simple Perpendicular style, all the better for the addition of its battlemented belfry.

Melbourne House

RCAHMS

11 Coral Bingo, 1936-8, D Paterson
A battered hulk (once La Scala cinema) and
now consigned to bingo, its magnificent stepped
slab tower tiled in cream and green used to
soar above Graham Avenue; a parapeted
quadrant forms the entrance foyer.
Incongruous, dramatic and disdained.

At **Duntocher** the Romans
located their last-but-one fort at
the west end of the Antonine
Wall. It was not a large station,
probably an acre and a half,
with only a few hundred
soldiers garrisoned.
Nevertheless, much has been
found – altars, vases, coins,
querns – and in *Goldenhill
Park*, just east of Roman Road,
the foundations of the rampart
constructed in the year AD 140
can be seen. From here the wall
crossed the Duntocher Burn by
a bridge long thought to be
*perhaps the most ancient in
Scotland*. Restored by Lord
Blantyre in 1772 it was given a
lithic inscription in Latin
recording how *This bridge was
built under the auspices of the
Emperor Titus Aelius
Antoninus Hadrianus
Augustus, father of his country,
by Quintus Lollius Urbicus, his
lieutenant...*
Groome, writing a hundred
years after this restoration, is
more sceptical about this
suggestion of a second century
date, noting that the bridge *has
been so often repaired as to
retain few or no indications of
its date, and very probably was
not otherwise Roman than in
having been built with stones
abstracted from a previous
Roman structure.*

*United Free Duntocher West
Church*

Elsewhere in the housing estates to the east
and west are a few churches, and fewer schools,
worth the detour. The orange brick and
12 coppered walls of the **Methodist Church**,
1978-80, Roxby, Park & Baird, perch above
Second Avenue. **St Margaret's Church**,
1972, Gillespie, Kidd & Coia, at **Sinclair
Street**, sinks back into the ground, its long low
walls of ochre brick disappearing into a banked
and planted landscape within which lies a
protected inner world. At **St Margaret's
Hospice**, East Barns Street, 1969, the same
architects have incorporated splayed fascias,
continuous bands of glazing over random hole-
in-the-wall windows, with wards designed in
an open-plan arrangement.

DUNTOCHER
There is still a vague sense of being in a village
street along Dumbarton Road, particularly
between Glenhead and West End House. At the
east end of **Old Mill Road**, a few rubble-
walled cottages recall the millworkers'
settlement that prospered here from the 1780s
until the American Civil War put an end to
cotton imports. But it takes time to find the
overgrown cleft of **Duntocher Burn** and a
good imagination to picture the sixteen water
wheels which once powered a burgeoning
textile industry. Nor is it easy to conjure up
that Radical community which combined
reforming politics with reformed religion –
except perhaps in the plain piended meeting
hall kirk of the **United Free Duntocher West
Church**, 1822, at the corner of Old Street.
Today's community has lost its local industry
though it is not without social and spiritual
succour. **Glenhead Community Centre**,
1967, on Duntiglennan Road, is a neatly
proportioned if somewhat dated assemblage of
brick and timber; the **Antonine Sports
Centre**, 1978, Jenkins & Marr, a more recent
shedded provision clad in dark stained panels
of oblique timber, advertises itself in boldly
painted yellow lettering.

Trinity Parish Church

Dick

Duntocher Trinity Parish Church,
1950-2, William Reid
Red brick religion gains most from a splendid
site looking down from Roman Road over the
valley of the Duntocher Burn. Parabola arches
in the entrance, transept gables and a lozenge-
windowed belfry produce period-piece
distinction.

St Mary's Church, 1954, Thomas Cordiner
Romanesque-derived forms in raw red
Accrington brick. In the campanile is the bell
from the original 1850 church.

St Joseph's Church, 1963-4,
Gillespie, Kidd & Coia
Hidden away in Faifley – where much
attractive rehabilitation of council housing is
underway – presbytery, hall and church group
around a forecourt opening out to the junction
of Lawmuir Crescent and Faifley Road. The
distinctive vocabulary of this practice is
everywhere evident in the manipulation of
light – at the transverse clerestorey over the
altar, along the curving walls of the baptistery
and Lady Chapel, and through the erratic hole-
in-the-wall windows of the hall. The materials
are facing brick externally with timber
windows and doors, with a copper-covered roof.

By eponymous coincidence
the fortunes of Duntocher owed
much to the enterprise of cotton
spinner William Dunn (1770-
1849). In 1808 Dunn purchased
the ailing mill at Duntocher,
one of the earliest in Scotland.
By introducing his own
machinery, Dunn began the
process of recovery. In 1811 he
bought Faifley Mill and in 1813
obtained Dalnottar Iron Works.
Milton Mill was built and in
1831 Dunn's holdings were
increased further with the
purchase of Highgate Mill.
Meanwhile, he had acquired
several local estates so that by
the time of his death not only
did he employ several thousand
people but he owned some 2000
acres of land, including more
than half of what would later
become the burgh of Clydebank.

Dick

St Joseph's Church

RCAHMS

Cochno House, *c.*1757, John Adam (?) (*above*)
A deep-plan, seven-bay pavilion-roofed house of unexceptional classical distinction. The pedimented two-storey-and-basement façade has a slightly overscale Roman Doric porch and there is a central splayed projection with balustraded parapet to the south. Extended in a lower kitchen block in 1842, the composition was imbalanced further by the later raising of the wing. More charming are the stable offices which form a U-plan around an open court.

Created originally by the Hamiltons of Barns the landscaped park and buildings of Cochno have been owned since 1956 by the University of Glasgow whose animal husbandry and astronomical departments now use the estate.

The Antonine Wall, begun in AD 142 or 143, traversed Scotland from Bo'ness on the Firth of Forth to Old Kilpatrick on the Clyde. Some 60 years earlier the Romans had penetrated north as far as the Highland Line, winning a major victory at Mons Graupius somewhere in the north-east, but by the middle of the second century AD the Emperor Antoninus Pius fixed the imperial border in central Scotland.

Unlike Hadrian's Wall, completed about 20 years earlier, the Antonine Wall was built not of stone but of earth and turf, though the underbuilding of the rampart was constructed of heavy stones. The army was billeted in forts about 2 miles apart of which 16 are at present known.

The Romans held the wall for only 15 years before retreating south to Hadrian's Wall. Later, however, they returned, renewing their occupation for some years. By the early years of the third century the Antonine Wall was finally abandoned.

Many relics and several highly decorative *distance slab* inscriptions have been found. These are preserved in the Hunterian Museum, University of Glasgow.

Edinbarnet House, 1885-9, J J Burnet
This is the fourth Edinbarnet, earlier houses on the site dating from 1644, 1758 and 1881, but even Burnet's Baronial mansion is incomplete. In 1975 a fire necessitated the removal of the third floor with disastrous impairment of the skyline. The parapeted corner keep and crow-stepped entrance wing remain but the absence of pitched roof, dormers and chimneys has fatally traduced the building's stylistic integrity.

OLD KILPATRICK
Between the Clyde and the A82 dual carriageway lie Old Kilpatrick and Bowling. North of the road, a few buildings are scattered on the

slopes of the Kilpatrick Hills. The high-pitched roof of **Clydebank Crematorium**, 1967, Sir Frank Mears & Partners, rakes its eaves above clerestorey glazing into a chimneyed tower at the east. **Glenarbuck House**, 1830 (?), is a splendidly sited mansion of considerable elegance – eaves cornice, good Roman Doric porch, pedimented tripartite windows – the whole robustly shouldered with conically hipped gable bows. Further west, past a neat **lodge** with red-tiled ogee cap, a long drive leads uphill passing the weir and ruined laundry at **Auchentorlie Burn** to reach the site of the former Auchentorlie House. Now a new low wide-spreading house enjoys the view south, with some armorial stonework from its more prestigious predecessor incorporated into the landscaping.

Glenarbuck House

Below, commuter and tourist speed by. Two thousand years ago, however, Old Kilpatrick was the end of the line, the last fort on the Romans' Antonine Wall. Two hundred years ago, Bowling, too, was a termination – or a beginning; the point at which the Forth & Clyde Canal joined the Firth of Clyde. Now it is almost as difficult to recapture any sense of the latter's commercial activity as it is to imagine the former as a military outpost.

Old Kilpatrick Bowling Parish Church, 1812, 1897

The parish is, indeed, old and the site probably that of an early Culdee church built towards the end of the first millennium. The present church is a three-bay nave with a tall pinnacled, battlemented and buttressed entrance tower. Tracery is plain, though the nave windows have stone transoms. In 1897 the chancel was extended awkwardly in a splayed east end.

Below *Old Kilpatrick Bowling Parish Church*. Bottom *Church Halls*

The graveyard has many interesting tombs including one from the early 17th century and a large unidentified stone *claimed to be the effigy of St Patrick* but more likely that of a medieval knight. The simple gabled **Hamilton Vault** incorporates some medieval fragments.

Across the road are the **Church Halls**, 1897, in a whimsical rather ecclesiastical vernacular of roughcast and red sandstone. There is a charming pyramid-roofed entrance with a monogram (*Rex Lux Lex Dux*) and, in the long buttressed hall which faces a riverside meadow, a peacock in the stained glass.

Top *Old Secession Church.*
Above *St Patrick's Church*

Canal House

Beneath the **Erskine Bridge**, 1967-71, Freeman Fox – elegant in the distant landscape but awesomely monstrous above the village – are two more churches. The **Old Secession Church**, 1795, now converted to residential use, retains its powerful small-windowed mass and steeply piended roof. **St Patrick's Church**, 1979-80, Nicholson & Jacobsen, hugs the ground in a pleasant composition of pitched roofs and roughcast walls given interest by the deep splays at windows and doors.

In a quiet backwater off **Station Road** the odd half-cone piended roof of **Lussett House**, 1868, rises from creeper-covered walls, while nearby is hidden treasure – the magnificent cast-iron porch of **Vieward**.

Old Kilpatrick's best housing is council-built. At **Gavinburn Place** and **Gavinburn Gardens**, 1924-5, roughcast cottage flats, gabled and piended, with brick plinths and surrounds, have a special art deco quality. Even more successful is **Hawcraig, 237-257 Dumbarton Road**, 1939, Joseph Weekes; the idiom is Scottish vernacular: gables, corbels, stepping ridges, conical turrets all combine in a brilliantly turned corner at Roman Crescent to mark the western end of the village.

BOWLING
Bowling Basin has a tired jauntiness: the canalside trim of locks and bascule bridges is not as fresh as it might be, the few yachts and launches hardly upmarket but, despite the superimposed weight of the railway arches, separating the inner basin from the river and hiding the pedimented gables of **Canal House**, *c.*1800, there is still a scarcely-to-be-suspected nautical lightheartedness about the spot.

Between road, railway, canal and river, development is, inevitably, linear. Late Georgian houses at the **Bay Inn** and at **49** and **53 Dumbarton Road**, and a grander example, **Oakbank**, *c.*1850, a gabled ashlar mansion with Roman Doric doorpieces, central façade chimney, eaves cornice and two good dormers. Later came rubble-built terraces: **85-87** Dumbarton Road, *c.*1870, has balcony ironwork above its four entrances. Finally, tenements, old and not so old, the most unusual being **Redrow**, 1894, at **15-17** Dumbarton Road, planar in English bond brick, rescued from dull economy by texture and patterning.

Glasgow Art Gallery & Museum

Bowling Church, 1869, is a low kirk in simple Gothic entered through a peaked porch. Alongside are the later rough-faced rubble **Church Halls** – note the whorled cast-iron light bracket. The **Village School**, 1861, again in rubble, has a crow-stepped porch added in 1906. The **Horse Shoe Bar**, a gabled *mélange* of black-and-white mock Tudor, contrasts with the white farm forms of **Littlemill Distillery**, *c.*1750; enlarged 1875.

Dunglass Castle, 14th, 16th and 19th centuries
Whether or not the Romans ever had an outpost here the site was, as Garnett observed, *well calculated to command the navigation of the Firth*. Sometime around the end of the 14th century the Colquhoun family built a walled stronghold; the ruinous shore wall still has its seagate access from the river. On the western flank is a crumbling turreted addition of the 16th century. From 1738, on the recommendation of the Commissioners of Supply *that some of the freestanes out of the old ruinous house of Dunglass ... be used in repairing the quay there*, quarrying of the fabric went on until, in 1812, the property passed to Buchanan of Auchentorlie. A domestic wing was built and it was reported that *great care is now taken of what remains by the proprietor, for which he deserves the gratitude of all lovers of the picturesque*.
    The artist Talwin Morris lived here from 1893 to 1899 and after him the Macdonald family, in-laws of Mackintosh and MacNair. Both Morris and Mackintosh enriched

Bowling, painted by Horatio McCulloch between 1830-50

Garnett, visiting the newly completed Forth & Clyde Canal at Bowling at the outset of his 1798 *Tour through the Highlands,* was much impressed by *this amazing work* which would reduce the time needed to transport goods between the east and west of the country and *will greatly conduce to the establishment of manufacturers* across Central Scotland: *Its extreme length from the Forth to the Clyde is thirty-five miles, beginning at the mouth of the Carron on the east, and ending in the Clyde near Kilpatrick, on the west coast ... It rises and falls 160 ft, by means of thirty-nine locks, twenty of which are on the east side of the summit, and nineteen on the west ... There are eighteen draw-bridges, and fifteen aqueduct bridges of considerable size ...*

Dunglass Castle

RCAHMS (George Washington Wilson)

Dunglass, 1818

Talwin Morris (1865-1911), who lived at Dunglass Castle from 1893 until 1899, exercised an important role in the evolution of the Glasgow Style through his position as Art Director in the publishing firm of Blackie & Sons. He was a close friend of Francis Newbery, Director of Glasgow School of Art, and The Four – Charles Rennie Mackintosh, Margaret and Frances Macdonald, and Herbert MacNair – and it was he who introduced his employer Walter Blackie to Mackintosh, a meeting which subsequently led to the building of The Hill House, Helensburgh. Despite his early apprenticeship as an architect, Morris's creative work concentrated on the decorative applied arts: metalwork, jewellery, stained glass, furniture and, especially, graphics; the tautly sinuous motifs introduced by Morris and his staff in the illustrations and bindings of Blackie's books have become collectors' items.

Dunglass with sophisticated interiors long since altered.

For all its inaccessibility in the Esso Oil Terminal – security is tight and the visitor must be escorted – this is a lovely spot: yew trees stand in the shadow of the old castle walls, an ivy-covered **doocot**, 17th century (?), perches on the battlements overlooking the water and the austere obelisk of the **Henry Bell Monument**, 1838, punches dramatically free of the mossy whin.

MILTON

As its name implies this is a textile village, its early prosperity dependent on the **Milton Burn**. Now a rather neglected stream, the burn flows quietly through the indifferent housing of 20th-century expansion. But uphill its tumbling power can still evoke memories.

1 **Milton Mill** (*left*)
By 1780 the bleaching and printing of calico were under way. In 1794 the waterwheel ran 40 powerlooms installed *supposedly at the suggestion of James Watt* – only the second such example of textile industrialisation in Scotland. By far the most unusual remains are two **ruinous towers** hidden in the trees near **Milton House**, one of five storeys, the other of three. Each battlemented tower has a splayed eastern façade of superimposed Gothicised Palladian windows, some blind, some given Gothick astragals. Amidst the trees it is all but impossible to imagine the high cotton mill that once linked these two structures. Attached to the south tower is a dormered cottage oddly endowed with both Gothick window and Georgian fanlight.

Back downhill by the Clyde what remains from earlier days is modest: **Clyde View**, 1888, has some tidy Renaissance detail and a good roof ventilator, while at **Milton Primary**

Left *Whyte's Corner.*
Above *Crannog Cottage Old Folks' Home*

School, 1905, the classical mouldings are heavier, and the roof ventilator splendidly baroque.

2 Commended by the Saltire Society, **Whyte's Corner**, 1937, Joseph Weekes, presents a roughcast crescent of two-storey flatted housing, a convincing amalgam of Scots vernacular and art deco. **Crannog Cottage Old Folks' Home**, 1953, has a distinctly 1950s feel, especially clear in its copper-covered segmental entrance canopy.

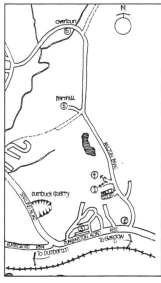

4 **Milton House**, *c*.1792 *(below)*
Through urn-topped gate-piers, a drive leads to the former mill manager's mansion. The two-storey-and-basement house is gabled and has an orthodox five-bay pedimented façade. There is a Roman Doric doorpiece approached by a short flying stair. Urns decorate the parapet of an otherwise plain but elegant façade.

Strikes by the mill workers of Milton during the autumn of 1833 and spring of 1834 brought serious social unrest to the village. Infantry soldiers were billeted in the Cotton Mill and dragoons quartered at Dumbarton; weavers, brought down from Glasgow as blackleg labour, had to be taught block printing by the proprietor of the Cotton Mill himself, Andrew Muter; the owner of the printworks, Patrick Miller, had to retreat to Glasgow for fear of his safety; at Muter's home, Milton House, the windows *were on one occasion knocked in under cloud of night* while at the printworks *on a dark winter night, to the music of fife, a lawless concourse of people smashed 300 panes of glass.* Conflict between soldiers and strikers was avoided but relationships were bitter.

5 **Barnhill House**, largely 19th century
Further up the valley past Loch Bowie is a much less composed grouping of two-storey buildings. From 1543 Barnhill was the seat of the Colquhouns of Milton and part of that early dwelling may be incorporated into what is now a pleasant accretion of Victorian hipped roofs and canted bays.

Overtoun House

It is one of the puzzles of archaeology that the twin-headed basalt plug of Dumbarton Rock should have yielded up no sure proof of early occupation. Seeming to disdain its impregnability, the Romans terminated their cross-Scotland wall some mile or two to the east. Why? Was the rock already in Caledonian hands? Or did the Romans invest it as some kind of combined port and forward post?

Many historians have found this second speculation irresistible, identifying the rock with Theodosia, capital of the Roman province of Valentia. Others dismiss this as unfounded or, indeed, ill-founded on a forged Latin history of the 18th century. But genuine documents, from the fifth century at the earliest, do substantiate the existence of a fortified settlement called Alcluith or Alt Clut or Ailcluaithe – Clyde Rock. Commanding both the Firth and the Vale of Leven route to the north, this was the stronghold of the British kingdom of Strathclyde – *Dun Breatann*, the fortress of the Britons, the Gaelic Scots to the north called it, adumbrating its name of Dumbarton.

Dumbarton Rock, and the castle on it, passed in and out of royal hands, the most dramatic attempts to wrest it back being made in the 16th century, first by Matthew, Earl of Lennox, in 1514 during the minority of James V, and again in 1543-4 when the next Earl, also Matthew, allied himself with the English King Henry VIII in an unsuccessful rebellion. In 1572, James VI awarded the Earldom to the Stewarts, a scion of this powerful family becoming the 1st Duke of Lennox in 1581. A century later the peerage devolved once more upon the Crown but by 1702 the entire patrimony of the Lennox line had been sold.

6 **Overtoun House**, 1859-63, James Smith
A Baronial Revival castle of colossal proportion built for the Rutherglen chemical manufacturer James White, whose son was to become the first Lord Overtoun. Overtoun's high tower, complete with corbelled battlements and mock cannon, commands the landscape for miles around. Close to, the approach is equally intimidating, a massive *porte-cochère* crushing the self-esteem of any visitor. White himself took a personal interest in much of the design, directing his architect to a variety of Baronial sources and instructing the raising of the main tower by an extra storey during construction. In 1895, H E Milner spanned the gorge of the **Overtoun Burn** with a superbly dramatic bulbously battlemented **bridge**.

The interiors by J Moyr Smith are of high quality, while beyond the terraced lawns there is a ruinous folly, a Nature Trail and hill-walking and climbing at the Lang Craigs. *Estate is open to the public.*

A **DUMBARTON ROCK**
The defences of Dumbarton Rock turn its twin crags into a safe citadel. Battlemented walls curtain precipitous cliffs while the steep defiles which climb up to the small plateau between the summits are protected by more developed fortifications. From the timber-laced ramparts of Alcluith to the Georgian batteries seen today, this pattern has remained unchanged.

King George's Battery, 1735, John Romer
Approached through the **Outer Gate**, 19th century, the Battery juts out to its corbelled sentinel box like the prow of some huge stone ship. The battery platform, part of General Wade's reconstruction of the Rock's southern defences, replaced the medieval ramparts seen

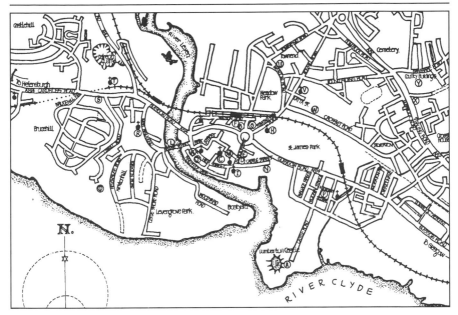

in Slezer's view of 1693, as the Governor's House did the great gatehouse.

Governor's House, 1735, John Romer
A three-storey-and-attic skew-gabled block erected on the site of the former round-towered gatehouse. The architecture is tough with little more than an open pediment and the texture of the rubble walls to relieve its austerity. The Governor's House and Battery are all but aligned on the same axis of symmetry.

West of the Governor's House a short length of wall, perhaps a remnant of a medieval hall, connects to the **Spur Battery** against which a **Lower Guard House**, 1735, was erected by Wade. Thereafter the **Back Wall** climbs

Governor's House

SDD

In 1803 Dorothy Wordsworth climbed the Rock with her brother William and their companion Coleridge. They found a ruined windmill, *Wallace's Sword* in the guardroom and an ancient trout trapped in the well. *This is a wild and melancholy walk on a blustering cloudy day: the naked bed of the river, scattered over with sea-weed; grey swampy fields on the other shore; sea-birds flying overhead; the high rock perpendicular and bare ...*

Dumbarton Castle drawn by Francis Place, c.1701

Glasgow Art Gallery and Museum

Dumbarton Castle: engraving by Slezer, 1693

Although Dumbarton is mentioned in a charter of 1238 as a Royal castle in the charge of the Earls of Levenax or Lennox, it was not until the expulsion of the Norsemen, 1262-6, that it began to develop any commercial importance as a port. Defence, however, remained the Rock's paramount virtue, and fortifications were on many occasions destroyed, rebuilt and further elaborated. In 1489, for example, James IV successfully laid siege to the castle recovering it from the hands of Lord Darnley, the rebellious son of the Earl of Lennox. Stability was short-lived and in the following century, particularly during the reign of Mary, the castle changed hands as pro-French and pro-English factions fought to dominate the temporal and spiritual affairs of Scotland. The first half of the 17th century proved no more settled so that by the time of the Restoration the castle was in serious disrepair. At length, as a result of the Union of 1707, Dumbarton became *one of the four garrisons in Scotland ... to be constantly kept in repair as a fortification* and improvements were made. These survived to be further reinforced by the strengthening of coastal defences during the Napoleonic Wars.

Dumbarton Castle

around the cliffs through the **Spanish Battery**, 1735, to terminate in the old **Bower Battery**, reconstructed 1735.

Above and behind the Governor's House, the **Guard House**, 16th century with 18th-century additions, has been squeezed between the cliffs to protect the ascent. Two gravestones with interlace decoration of the 10th or 11th century are kept here. Steps continue to climb in the defile to reach the tall **Portcullis Arch**, 14th century (?), *the most ancient surviving structure on the Rock*. Above its pointed arch vault it provides a bridge link below **The Beak** summit to the east and the **White Tower Crag** to the west, while below the path continues to the high ground at the heart of the Rock. Though this must have been the site of earliest occupation, only the ancient **well** and **French Prison**, *c*.1760, can be found today.

Duke of York's Battery, *c*.1795
Built to encase the ruinous North Entry, it incorporates the vaulted cellar of the medieval

Wallace Tower which, until the 18th century, rose four storeys providing flanking defence of the northern approach. That Wallace himself was incarcerated here has been doubted, but it is certainly true that the Castle's governor, Sir John Graham of Menteith – *fause Menteith*– was prominent in effecting his capture in 1305.

From the old North Entry, walls girdle the north and east sides of the Rock. These are largely the work of the 1790s, the **Duke of Argyll's Battery** replacing the older Bellhouse Battery and the **Prince of Wales Battery** being built on the site of the 16th-century Round Battery. About 50m before the eastern wall ends above the rocks is another of Romer's sentinel box turrets.

Powder Magazine, 1748, William Skinner
Located in a walled enclosure on **The Beak**, this simple gabled building held gunpowder. Designed to resist bombardment, it has a thick barrel-vaulted structure, double doors and indirect ventilation openings.

DUMBARTON

The prosperity of medieval Dumbarton, chartered by Alexander II in 1221, owed as much to the sea connections afforded by the Clyde and the landward route north through the Vale of Leven as it did to the protection of the Rock. James IV, turning the port into a naval station in his pacification of the Western Isles, established shipbuilding on the Leven and stimulated local trade. And when in 1609 James VI confirmed the town's burgh status, he authorised three annual fairs to be held – an indication that Dumbarton had become the principal market town of north Clyde.

By the 18th century Dumbarton was Scotland's largest producer of glass; the three tall cones of the glassworks kilns rose above the town's skyline like man-made responses to the Rock. By 1850 there were four shipyards, two for *the construction of ironships. Slater's Directory* of 1852 noted that *no other town in Britain can surpass Dumbarton in this line of business.* The number of yards rose to six; by 1900 around 5000 men were employed. Bolstered by engineering, shipbuilding remained Dumbarton's major industry until the middle of the present century.

Medieval Dumbarton survives in
B fragmentary form. The **College Bow**, *c.*1453,

Below *Survey Map 1818.*
Bottom *College Bow*

DUMBARTON

Aerial view, town centre

Using kelp from the Western Isles, the Dixon family built an industry surpassed only by the shipbuilding enterprise of the Dennys in the later 19th century. Over 300 workers were employed and, if *Pigot's Directory* of 1825-6 can be believed, as much as £120,000 paid in annual customs duty. But by 1831 a sudden decline had set in *in consequence of the decease of the principals engaged together in this business.*

Ralston Photography

is an isolated pointed arch remnant from the Collegiate Chapel of the Blessed Virgin Mary, a semi-monastic foundation of the 15th century created, under papal mandate, by Lady Isabella Lennox. The church did not escape the Reformation and, when its ruins were removed by railway construction in the 19th century, the single arch was erected in Kirk Vennel, 1850, and later rebuilt, 1907, on its present site beside the Municipal Buildings (see p.26).

Across the Leven, which divided the ancient parishes of Dumbarton and Cardross, stood the **Old Parish Church of Cardross**. Little more than a simple rectangular cell, it continued in use until 1644. Its ruined walls – one an ivy-covered blind arcade of three First Pointed arches – can be discovered in Levengrove Park. Buried here are members of the Dixon family who owned Dumbarton Glassworks and lived in nearby Levengrove House, *c.*1780, dem. *c.*1880.

Below *Old Parish Church of Cardross*. Bottom *Dumbarton Glassworks, c.1800*

Dick

Dumbarton District Libraries

TOWN CENTRE

C **College Way**, 1969, Garner, Preston & Strebel
The formula – cantilevered concrete canopies
above which exposed flint panels are separated
by slot windows – has been repeated along
College Way and around the Town Square
imparting consistent character to this newly
contrived urban space. But the uniform
treatment, varied by an additional storey on
the north and the now tawdry wall of **North
Church**, 1878, John McLeod, is a little *too*
consistent. Certainly, shuttered concrete and
dull blue-red brick paviors numb the senses,
despite the flurry of a few trees. A pity Robert
Napier's 1824 marine engine, which formerly
stood in a small pool, can no longer be enjoyed;
it was removed to the town's East End (see
p.31).

Below *College Way.* Middle
Masonic Temple. Bottom *Burgh
Halls*

Dick

The **Denny Civic Theatre**, 1969, brings no
relief: a dark brick box with misplaced rhetoric
focused on a brutalist concrete escape stair.
Dark again, but finely massed and detailed if
grimly inscrutable, the **Masonic Temple**,
1973-4, Garner, Preston & Strebel, is the
outstanding new building east of the Square.

Dick

D **Burgh Hall**, 1865-6, 1883, Melvin & Leiper
Designed by William Leiper as Burgh Hall and
Library, the building has had a succession of
differing uses: academy, school of art, primary
school, police offices, electricity offices,
education offices. The style is a forceful French
Gothic, the composition symmetrical. At the
centre a pinnacled belfry stands forward, rising
140 ft in four stages above an arched porch. A
fire in 1882 destroyed much of the roofing
including the belfry spire. Leiper's restoration,
1883, added dormers but left the belfry as it
was. In 1976 the halls at the rear fell victim to
another fire. In 1984, Strathclyde Region
Architects replaced them with a smart
buttressed blockwork box.

Dick

25

Top *Sheriff Court House.*
Above *Risk Street Housing*

E **Sheriff Court House**, 1824-6,
J Gillespie Graham & Robert Scott
A pavilion-roofed Georgian mansion built as
the County Buildings: three bays of coupled
Ionic pilasters sitting on a rusticated ground
floor support entablature and pediment.
Balustraded wings, added by William Spence
in 1865, extend the façade along its rusticated
base. Extensions on the north and south, 1895
and 1898 – the latter with a fine Venetian
window – are by D McNaughton, the low
courtyard block between by Halley & Neil,
1906. All that remains of Dumbarton Prison
(dem.1973) is a handsome entrance portico *in
its original position and incorporated in the
new boundary wall* behind the Sheriff Court.
Above the round-arched doorway is a square
plaque displaying the town's elephant-and-
castle coat of arms.

Church Street marks out a clear eastern
edge to the Town Centre just as its
predecessor, Kirk Vennel, did in medieval
times. **Risk Street Housing**, 1965-70, Garner,
Preston & Strebel, creates no streets, but the
five- and six-storey flatted blocks are set in
generously planted landscape, their varied
glazing, balcony balustrading and step section
profile combining to preclude monotony.

F **Municipal Buildings**, 1900-3,
James Thomson
The Scottish flavour continues in good red
sandstone – more Jacobean that Baronial. The
bartizaned tower on the south has a French
roof; that to the east four tourelles and two
flanking chimney stacks to protect its tall
leaded ogee. In the grounds is the open portal
of the College Bow (see p.23).

Strathleven Place follows the old road to
Dumbarton Mill. A few early Victorian houses
remain: **Drumoyne**, 1853, J T Rochead, in
mild Tudor Gothic; **Deveron House**, *c.*1866,
pavilion-roofed with bracketed eaves, very
plain but very good; and the District Council's
Housing Department, formerly Mansefield
House, 1837, similar but gabled and much
traduced.

Public Library

G **Public Library**, 1909-10, William Reid
Not a large building, but grand: a rusticated
assemblage of Renaissance elements. Its blank,
factory-like extension is, however, appalling –
though it does incorporate a lintel stone, dated

1732 and 1790, taken from the former
Mackenzie mansion in High Street to be set
gracelessly above an emergency exit.

H **St Patrick's Church**, 1900-3, Dunn & Hanson
The nave-and-aisle church in rough-faced red
sandstone came first. Begun in pointed idiom,
the style changes to Late Decorated in the later
detached tower, 1926-7, Pugin & Pugin, a tall
belfry whose hefty angle buttresses reduce to
crocketed pinnacles above a battlemented
parapet. Inside is a statue, *St Michael the
Archangel*, by Eric Gill.

St Patrick's Church

High Street

HIGH STREET: South

The High Street perpetuates its medieval
alignment: following the sweep of the Leven at
a short vennel distance, it swung round from
the Parish Church, past the ferry crossing and
on to Townhead, beyond which the tidal flood
plain made building impossible. The kirk is
still there, though not the original post-
Reformation church. The ferry has gone,
superseded by **Dumbarton Bridge** (see p.30)
in the 18th century. In 1798 Garnett noted that
the greatest part of the buildings are antique
but since then much has changed, especially
during the 1960s when the backlands down the
old rig feus to the river were cleared and the
vennel slums to the north-east transformed
into a new **Town Centre**.

Riverside Parish Church

I **Riverside Parish Church**, 1811, John Brash;
renovated 1908
Built to replace the 17th-century parish kirk,
steeple and pedimented gable command the
westward curve of High Street. Classically
severe, there is a *pressed-in* portico to the west
and a large segmental window to the east.
Urns perch on the belfry and adorn the
gatepiers to the kirkyard. The interior,

refurbished 1886, has its Presbyterian clock on the gallery face, here set between burgh arms and burning bush.

Some old gravestones can be found in the churchyard but parked cars and cramped new halls, 1975-6, destroy any sense of the sacred. The few weeping trees seem appropriate.

Glencairn Greit House

Dumbarton District Libraries

J **Glencairn Greit House**, 1623
A last survivor of the aristocratic town house, this was the urban home of the Earls of Glencairn and later the Dukes of Argyll. Now the oldest building in the street, changes in the masonry suggest it may have been completed on the basis of some even earlier structure. Between tall crow-stepped gables it rises three floors, the attic having four finely pedimented eaves dormers. To the left is the low arch of **Quay Pend** leading to the river; the three higher arches of the street arcade were formed 1924-5.

Bank of Scotland (detail)

Dick

Hiram Walker's Distillery, 1937-8, overwhelms the Parish Church. Seven storeys and as many buildings, all in bright red brick – at the time of construction the biggest distillery in Europe – its omnipresent bulk, replacing shipyard cranes and sheds, testifies to the role of whisky in the town's economy.

At 3 High Street are the former head offices, 1881-8, of **Hiram Walker (Scotland) PLC**, three storeys of classically moulded ashlar. Next door the pink sandstone of the **Bank of**

Scotland, 1897, J Dick Peddie & George Washington Browne, is cut in Late Gothic detail with corbelled canted bays to the first and second floors. The opposite corner of Riverside Lane is turned in more Modern manner by the **Royal Bank of Scotland** (**No 37**), two aggressively horizontal glazed storeys overhung by cream-tiled fascias. Unassuming mid-Victorian façades in painted ashlar exist at **43-45** and **107-109**, all with moulded surrounds and eaves cornice. At **53** a five-bay front is enhanced by three bays of fluted pilasters, with coats of arms incorporated into the capitals; a narrow façade, 1895, rises four storeys with a half-timbered gable oversailing the bays below.

Dumbarton's High Street is rich in provincial art deco. Before some crude alteration, **City Bakeries**, 1926, at **55-59** had a splendid first floor in cream with green-tiled fins to symmetrical glazing, decorative inset tiles and a jagged frieze. On the corner of Quay Street is **Burton's**, 1937-8, which replaced the old Elephant Hotel, 1762, with white faience, and at **97-99** the buff façade of **Woolworths**, 1939, similar in style with stepped parapet and finned mullions.

K **High Church**, 1863-4, John Honeyman Early English Gothic; a lanceted gable front with jamb shafts and mullions of black Carnock stone. The building now functions as the **Bell Leisure Centre** with none-too-fortunate ancillary accommodation down Riverside Lane. The corner of **Brewery Lane** however, is properly accented by a tall lance-like spire closing the curve of the High Street with an echo of the Parish Church steeple to the east.

Top, middle & above *Art deco in the High Street*
High Church

North of Bridge Street is the **Artizan**, a flat riverside site on which, from c.1777 to 1830, the three great cones or kilns of Dumbarton Glassworks dominated the town's economy and its skyline. Redevelopment in the 1960s cleared the ground for the dual carriageway of the A814 leading to the new **Artizan Bridge**, 1973-4.

Leven Embankment
Here a transformation has occurred: backlands dereliction has been cleared to create an attractive promenade passing beside carefully

Leven Embankment

Dumbarton Bridge

planted islands of car parking. Pleasure craft in mid-stream and the prospect of Levengrove Park make the quay a place to enjoy. Some of the views downriver are still too squalid while along the High Street Backs there is not yet enough new riverside building, though Garner, Preston & Strebel's improvements, 1963, 1972, promised much. Nor did they forget the needs of the moment for nearby are what must be the finest **public toilets**, 1963, north of the Clyde.

Dumbarton Bridge, 1765, John Brown
Long planned, the crossing of the Leven was not achieved until the 18th century. The bridge is supported on five segmental arches on fat cutwater piers. In 1884 W R Copeland widened the carriageway with iron cantilevers. Further reconstruction was effected 1933-4.

HIGH STREET: North
On the northern side of the High Street the old feuing pattern, which for centuries determined plot size and thus façade width, has been abandoned to accommodate the edge of new Town Centre shops and offices. Earlier infill had anticipated this change in elevational proportions: at **112** the **Dumbarton Equitable Co-operative Society** had replaced several older properties with a broad symmetrical front, while before that at **82-90**, 1895, a stringcourse-stressed tenement range replaced

four 17th-century gable-fronted houses, the
infamous *Holy Land* on the corner of College
Street.

At the eastern end of the street similar
exchanges were repeated. Another tenement
range was erected at **4-6**, 1898, with some
unusually decorative panels below the second-
floor sills, and at **24-32**, 1938, more **Co-
operative** shops and halls, again wide-fronted,
symmetrical and in muted art deco.

Narrow façades are rare: an older tenement
at **16-20**, 1879, crested with timber dormers;
and at **12**, the three bays of Eric Sutherland's
TSB, formerly the Savings Bank of Glasgow,
1938, tall simplified windows decidedly elegant
but for the later crude addition of a box fascia.

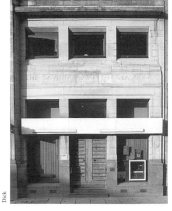

M **St Augustine's Episcopal Church**,
1873, R Rowand Anderson
An ashlar gable in Decorated Gothic fronts the
five-bayed aisled nave. Behind is *a beautifully
proportioned interior*, one of Anderson's best.
There is a parsonage to the north, also by
Anderson, and a linking hall added in 1907 by
A C Denny.

NEWTOWN: East End
Dumbarton's East End is the industrial part of
town. The world's first civilian **Ship Model**
N **Experiment Tank**, 1882-3, designed for
Denny's by E R Mumford & J McQuorn
Rankine, still remains behind a polychromatic
gable façade on **Castle Street**. Located nearby
is the marine engine Robert Napier designed
for the paddle-steamer *Leven* in 1824. Today,
the town's economy no longer depends on
labour-intensive heavy industry but on more
passively generated wealth. From the huge
brick bulk of the distillery that dominates the
end of the High Street as far as the edge of
town at Dumbuck, acres of riverside land are
given over to the storage of whisky. Even the
visitor to the castle must pass twenty
warehouse gables down the long straight line of
Castle Road.

But the industrial character of the East End
is as much to be judged from the tenements of
Glasgow Road and Knoxland, built to house the
shipyard workers a century or so ago, as it is
from these bleak compounds of bonded storage.

A few houses on **Glasgow Road** recall a
suburban character that antedates industrial
expansion: **67-69**, early 19th century, now the

Top *12 High Street*. Above *St
Augustine's Episcopal Church*

In 1938 the **Blackburn
Aircraft Factory** opened on
the site of the former Barge
Park close to the Leven
Shipyard. During the Second
World War production
concentrated on the Sunderland
Flying Boat – about 250 were
manufactured – but in 1945 the
factory began to produce
prefabricated aluminium
houses. In October 1945 the
first aluminium prefab to be
erected in Scotland was built at
Smollett Road, Dumbarton. By
the time the firm closed in 1960
some 12,000 prefab houses had
left the Blackburn factory.

Dumbuck Hotel

Shipbuilding at the mouth of the Leven might be said to date from when James IV (1488-1513) fitted out his fleet here for the subjugation of the Western Isles. But it is with the enterprise of the Denny family in the 19th century that the industry is properly associated.

In 1814 William Denny built the *Marjory* as a rival to Henry Bell's *Comet*. It became the first steamboat to cross the English Channel. A generation later in 1844 four of William's sons – William, Alexander, Peter and James – founded Wm Denny & Brothers and the firm *soon gained a reputation for their iron-hulled ships* as well as the manufacture of boilers and engines. At first the Denny yard was on the west side of the river but in 1867 the Leven shipyard on the east was built. By the 1880s the yard stretched from Castle Street downriver as far as the Rock.

The *Cutty Sark*, the last and one of the fastest of the great clippers, was completed by Dennys in 1869. As steam replaced sail, Dennys kept ahead of the times. In 1879 they built the world's first steel-hulled vessel, in 1901 the first turbine-powered passenger liner, and in 1934 the first all-welded ship.

In the best tradition of Victorian philanthropy the Denny legacy to Dumbarton was considerable: their individual mansion houses, Levengrove Park, Dennystown housing scheme (now gone) and Knoxland Square.

Knoxland

District Council Planning Office, is a pavilion-roofed block with eaves cornice and good attic dormers, formerly two houses each with its pilastered doorpiece; **87**, **89** and **91** vary the theme of cottage villa; and **Dumbuck Hotel**, 1824, remodelled 1923, despite much alteration and recent extension, still provokes a memory of its country house origins. But tenements and terraces predominate. Elsewhere, Glasgow Road is strongly urban: three-storey with coupled canted bays at **200-216**, 1898, and a storey higher at **129-165**, 1906, terminating beside the railway bridge in a conically capped bow-windowed corner. More characteristic, however, are **96-108**, where crow-stepped chimneyed gables rise from a flat façade.

Knoxland, 1873-90

Between the early 1870s and 1890, Peter Denny and the Dumbarton Building Society undertook a programme of house building centred on the new open space of Knoxland Square. Three-storey tenements in droved ashlar, with turnpike stairs at the rear and street elevations on the crow-step gable model were built at **15-27 Castlegreen Street**, **3-7 Victoria Street** and **1-13 Knoxland Square**, 1882-4, while a plainer variety appeared at **1-11 Castlegreen Street**, **5-27 Wallace Street** and **2-24 Victoria Street**. For middle management, rows of terraces or close-packed semi-detached were built on **Wallace Street**, **Bruce Street** and along the south side of **Knoxland Square**. A workers' kirk, **Knoxland Parish Church**, 1884, dem. 1986, was also erected and a school – replaced in 1974 by **Knoxland Primary School** on Glasgow Road, a long horizontal grouping of white fascias and clerestorey glazing. Knoxland retains its coherence of architectural style and urban form, although gaps and replacements have occurred. At **12-14 Wallace Street**, for example, there are some three-storey brick and cement-render flats with *Mayan* stair towers lit by glass blocks. Yet this still remains one of Dumbarton's most valuable enclaves of consciously designed townscape. There is little from more recent times to match it. Only perhaps on the other side of Glasgow Road along the leafy terraces of **Silverton Avenue** and **Overtoun Avenue** is there any kind of comparably controlled order.

Silverton Avenue

WEST END

Across Dumbarton Bridge the droved ashlar tenements of **3-7 Clyde Shore Road**, 1888, curve up to **Levengrove Park**. The Park, gifted to the town in 1885 by shipbuilders John McMillan and Peter Denny was, until 1861, the estate of the glass-making Dixon family whose thirty-room house Levengrove House, *c*.1780, had looked down over the Leven for a hundred years or so until its demolition in 1880. Today, the Dixons are remembered in the ruins of the Old Cardross Kirk (see p.58). A jaunty **Park Lodge**, 1884-5, in whimsical Tudorbethan, its stuccoed gable bracketed out over a bay window, sets the mood for lighthearted leisure.

Kirktonhill

Laid out in the 1870s, uphill and upwind from the centre of town, many of its large detached houses, particularly along Dixon Drive, are the work of local architect John MacLeod. **Methlan Park House**, 1880-1, which has a four-stage Italianate tower and two-storey pilastered bow window looking south across the Firth, is MacLeod's. **Garmoyle**, 1890, since 1934 a Carmelite monastery, is by Burnet Son & Campbell – red roofed, ruggedly rambling Baronial in raked-joint rubble.

Above *Methlan Park House.*
Left *Garmoyle*

Stables, Helenslee

Helenslee, 1866-70, John Honeyman
Honeyman inflated an earlier house by J T
Rochead into a massive mansion climbing
through three and four storeys to a French-
roofed tower fit for the shipbuilding baron
Peter Denny: delicate balcony ironwork,
balustraded parapets and Honeyman's refined
Q stonework detailing. In 1926 **Keil School**
transferred here from Southend in Argyll. The
Gothick stables block, 1865, also by Honeyman,
has become a technical wing.

Levenford House, 1853, J T Rochead
As one of the subscribers to the publication of
Robert Billings's *The Baronial and
Ecclesiastical Antiquities of Scotland* (1845-52),
Rochead had Scottishness fresh in his mind
when another of the Denny dynasty, James,
commissioned this magnificent pile. From cap
house to cable moulding the house engrosses
all the Baronial elements which Billings had
illustrated, the hillside wonderfully exploited
with battlemented garden walls, turreted
portal, stables, 1865, and lodge-house all
contributing to the fortified fancy. Particularly
creative is the quirky step-canted gabled bay
on the south front. The property serves today
as the headquarters of Dumbarton District
Libraries. Fortunately, despite internal
adjustments, the high quality of woodwork and
stained glass is largely unimpaired.

Across **West Bridgend** from James Denny's
mansion was **Dennystown**, a shipyard
workers' suburb of two-storey flatted houses
built beside the Leven in 1853. Rochead was
again the architect and William Denny,
James's brother, the client. The gridded streets
have all gone, replaced by three 16-storey point
blocks, 1970.

Below *West Bridgend Church.*
Bottom *Bruce's Stables*

R **West Bridgend Church**, 1887-8,
John MacLeod
The symmetrical gable with its large wheel
window is in well-intentioned Gothic, but just a
little dull. The **Church Hall**, 1860, William
Spence, is better: a former church, it is
arranged on an L-plan pinned by a sculptural
broach spire rising above the porch.

S **Bruce's Stables**, late 18th century,
Charles Ross
An intriguing limewashed wall of three
Gothick gables full of neo-medieval *naïveté* –

blind ogees, blind gunloops, battlemented skews, clustered shafts and quoins. The implied connection with King Robert Bruce is wishful thinking for the three (now two) cottages were built for Easter Hole, later Braehead Farm.

T On Cardross Road is **St Michael's Church**, 1952, by Gillespie, Kidd & Coia; a long red brick nave with diamond-shaped windows and a tall glazed tower with grillage belfry.

St Michael's Church

Past **Notre-Dame High School**, 1968, Boissevain & Osmond, six long horizontal storey-stripes of glazing, is **Dumbarton Joint Hospital**, 1898. The administration block is residential in scale but not so Georgian as it looks at first – the raised pedimented unit at the centre has vestigial scrolls and a doorway all dimly reminiscent of baroque church fronts. Religious allusions at the **Church of Jesus Christ of Latter Day Saints**, 1963-4, are confined to a needle spire.

Below *Joint Hospital.* Bottom *Braehead Primary School*

TOWNEND
In 1850 the Bowling/Dumbarton/Balloch railway connection skirted the northern edge of town. Opened in 1854, **Central Station** was altered to its present attractive form in 1896. The entrance is now under the railway bridge where, behind Gothic tracery and past the cusped panelling of the old ticket office, *c.*1900, stairs rise to track level above.

Across **Meadow Park** are two buildings, located to good effect on rising ground. The **Cottage Hospital**, 1890, Shiells & Thomson, responds to its good fortune with a pyramid-roofed tower, polychromatic sandstone and pedimented dormers. Across the road the high, wide and severely handsome façade of
U **Braehead Primary School**, built in 1914 by McWhannell & Rogerson as Dumbarton

35

Free High Church

Academy, stretches out above tiered grassy banks. The façade relies on rhythm rather than ornament, but there are three richly carved timber ventilators perching on the roof like baroque tempiettos. Replacing the Brock Memorial Baths of 1914, the recently completed **Meadow Sports & Leisure Centre** could have presented friendlier façades to both street and park.

Bonhill Road runs north from Central Station, first between bayed tenements and then through villa-land towards **Stirling Road**. Easy to overlook are the Health Board Offices in **Westonlee House**, *c.*1820, a Late Georgian mansion with a good Roman Doric doorpiece and small central pediment. Similar, with ground-floor canted bays, is **Hartfield House**, *c.*1830, on the corner of **Latta Street**.

V **Free High Church**, 1907-8, Halley & Neil A six-bay nave fronts **Latta Street** in an awkwardly narrow façade gable which bears the dates 1843-1908, making it clear that this is not the first church building of a Disruption congregation. This second kirk has its tower, too – a neat Arts & Crafts belfry with overhanging eaves between battlemented corner parapets.

At **46 Bonhill Road**, the grocery built by **Dumbarton Equitable Co-Operative Society**, 1934-5, is in gayer, art deco mood, especially evident in the undulating motifs along the wall to **Round Riding Road**.

W **Dumbarton Academy**, 1935-7, Joseph Weekes
Beginning as the burgh grammar school, the Academy has a long history which dates back to the 15th century and probably earlier. Not until 1972 was the move made to Crosslet Road to occupy Hartfield School. The original buildings – a wide two-storey pitched roof spread with splayed wings – are easily recognisable: *no money has been spent in needless ornamentation*, but they are still the most coherent piece of architecture in what has become a complex aggregation of classrooms and workshops. Nearby **St Patrick's Primary School**, 1971-2, by County Architect R Sutherland, is a single-storey spread in brown facing brick; monopitch classroom roofs pleasantly vary the skyline.

Dumbarton Academy

STIRLING ROAD

The Stirling Road (A82) runs north-west from
Milton, passing below the great whin cleft of
Dumbuckhill Quarry before it plunges through
those vast tracts of housing which now extend
Dumbarton's boundaries to the Old Kilpatrick
Hills. To the left, in Silverton, are the pre-war
schemes; on **Drumbuie Avenue**, **White
Avenue** and **Dumbuck Road** all the bold
Modernism of curved corner windows,
verandas, balconies, and horizontal glazing
patterns now compromised by pitched roof
alteration. To the right, in Bellsmyre, the
anonymity of more recent streets contours the
hillside.

Crosslet House, 1858, manages to survive
secluded in landscaped grounds. An attractive
but unexceptional sprawling mansion, built for
one Humphrey Campbell, its greatest asset is a
columned porch set obliquely against the
X house. More prominent, **West Overtoun
House**, 1895, J Thomson, adduces every kind
of Baronial effusion to attract attention. It may
be bombastic, but it is certainly more enjoyable
than the bland two-dimensional geometries of
the **Police Headquarters**, 1967, Dumbarton
County Architects, which lie behind.

Y **Strathclyde Regional Offices**, 1962-5,
Lane, Bremner & Garnett
Won in competition in 1960, buildings and
landscape intersect cleverly in plan and
section. A five-storey office block with pergola
parapet oversails a through driveway; a raised
council chamber acts as *porte-cochère*.

Above *West Overtoun House.*
Left *Strathclyde Regional
Offices*

Towards the end of the 19th century, Leighton wrote of the Leven: *on its beautiful banks are seen villages and public works, seats of gentlemen, embowered among ancient wood, lovely meadows, and lands rich with the labours of agriculture.*

Dalquhurn Cottage, early 19th century; once the works manager's home, is a conglomerate of the classical and the castellated with a semi-octagonal veranda redolent of *cottage orné* models, and **Dalquhurn House**, was home of the Smolletts until 1762, the year the family built workers' houses beside the bleachworks and named the new village Renton after their daughter-in-law Cecilia Renton, have both gone.

Football has always been a consuming passion in the Vale. In the late decades of the 19th century nineteen teams such as Renton, Vale of Leven and Dumbarton dominated the Scottish scene, winning the Scottish Cup frequently and often providing more than half the players in the national side.

In 1888 Renton FC won the Scottish Cup and went on to challenge the English cup-winners West Bromwich Albion. Winning this match, Renton were proclaimed *Champions of the World*, an achievement commemorated for many years on a signboard on the Club's pavilion at Tontine Park until the ground became the site of a local housing scheme.

The title of world champions did not, however, prevent Renton's defeat by Vale of Leven in the 1888 Dunbartonshire Cup Final. Much piqued by this embarrassment Renton lodged a number of protests with the Association including complaints about *the incompetency of the umpires* and *the hostility of the crowd*, a course of action which prompted the *Lennox Herald* to remark that *The Renton ... are not taking their defeat like men.*

Dalmoak House

VALE OF LEVEN

Ironically, the very purity of the River Leven sealed its fate. Attracted by the flood plain of the valley and the clean fresh water pouring down from Loch Lomond, the bleaching and printing industries established themselves here as early as 1715. At Dalquhurn *Hollan cloth is wonderfully whitened*, wrote McUre in 1736; but the very whiteness of the cloth seemed to blind people's perception of the change in the river. In the late 18th century attempts were made to mitigate pollution from the re-entrant lades, but to little effect.

At first, the adverse consequences were below the surface – no more salmon or trout – while above the waterline signs of prosperity were everywhere. A century later, the picture is reversed. While the Leven recovers, the banks of the river bear the scars of industrial dereliction, the country houses have gone or struggle for survival and the towns of the Vale endure the hopeful trauma of renewal.

RENTON
Dalmoak House, 1866-9

On the western slopes of the Vale of Leven, this large mansion in pompous castellated Gothic is no longer a private residence. It has a five-bay façade of coupled windows, corbelled battlemented parapets and a central tower rising behind. Hood-moulded lintels are everywhere – except in the oddly traceried arches of three staircase windows exposed at the rear by the U-plan. Inside and out the house is ubiquitously inscribed with the monogram of its first owner, James Aitken. At the stables, the central of three crow-stepped gables is raised as a doocot.

Renton, wrote the *Dumbarton Herald* in 1851, was *dragged out of public obscurity by the railway*. It seems to have slipped back into quiescent gloom. The **Dalquhurn Works**, a thriving centre for bleaching, printing and dyeing, have disintegrated into crumbling warehouses on a bend in the Leven.

In the late 19th century Renton grew in flatted red sandstone rows; many have been demolished but several on **Main Street** at **Woodvale**, at **259-265**, 1884, **283-295** and **307-319**, 1883, and in **John Street**, **Leven Street** and **Alexander Street** show the characteristic variations. Earlier dwellings are found: at **18-22 Main Street** and **Glenlyon**, *c.*1860, on the corner of Cardross Road, two-storey with pilastered or columned doorpieces; and at **Argyle Cottage** and **North Cottage**, single-storey, skew-gabled houses in ashlar.

Most housing is more recent, maintaining low scale. Roughcast tenements by Joseph Weekes at **216-222 Main Street** have a more robust urban feel, their severity relieved by canted close entries and convex windows set beneath an oversailing eaves at the ends of each block. Similar chamfer detail in the red sandstone of **Forestvil**, *c.*1890, **Alexander Street**.

Smollett Monument, 1774
A tall Tuscan column honouring the physician and novelist Tobias Smollett, rising 60 ft over the stepped monopitches of **Renton Primary School** to dominate the Main Street. The inscription is in part by Dr Samuel Johnson. Beside the column is a silver-painted cast-iron **fountain**, 1886, its cast reminder to *Keep the Pavement Dry* now redundant.

Public buildings are few. The **Victoria Institute**, 1887, on Main Street has a two-storey square bay with a good eaves cornice above. On Alexander Street, the **Masonic Temple** is more classical: a pilastered front with triple windows and soffit blocks on its eaves. Both are in red sandstone.

Renton Trinity Parish Church, 1891-2, H & D Barclay
The church sits above the Leven locked on the axis of Leven Street by its pinnacled tower. Beneath is a step-battlemented gable behind which a T-plan develops east into low wide-spreading transepts. Despite the width the style is Perpendicular.

Tobias George Smollett (1721-71), educated in Dumbarton, began his career apprenticed to a surgeon. Following a move to London in 1739, he took ship for the West Indies, settled in Jamaica but returned in 1744 to London where he practised, unsuccessfully, as a physician. Throughout these early years he wrote much and began to find fame when he turned the experience of his travels to account in a two-volume novel *The Adventure of Roderick Random*, 1748. This success laid the basis for a series of satirical picaresque novels much influenced by Cervantes and by no means unrelated to his own restless style of life. His output, as a translator and historian as much as a writer of fiction, was voluminous, not to say long-winded.

Below *Smollett Monument*. Bottom *Renton Trinity Parish Church*

Millburn Free Church

Dick

Smollett's Fountain marks the site of the *Old Oak Tree* which stood for many years at the junction of Main Street and Ferry Loan (later Bank Street) before it was cut down in 1865. So important had the tree been in Alexandria's community life, acting as the resort of orators, both religious and political, that its passing was marked by an obituary in the *Dumbarton Herald* of 12 Oct. Lamenting the elimination of this *village rostrum* the writer hoped *that those who issued the warrant for its execution will see fit to erect a drinking fountain or a pulpit for itinerant open-air orators, or some such fitting memorial object* .... Five years later Alexandria got its fountain and the local tradition for a time was sustained.

At the other end of town is another more Scottish, T-plan kirk in an earlier pointed idiom. Abandoned among its kirkyard graves, **Millburn Free Church**, 1843-5, by G M Kemp (?), is distinguished by its exceptional steepled entrance, a crude but unique confection of buttresses and pinnacles.

ALEXANDRIA

Like Renton, Alexandria is a product of the bleaching, printing and dyeing industries which packed the banks and bends of the Leven. Known originally as *The Grocery* it was only in the 19th century that it took its name from the local laird, Alexander Smollett.

The decisive element shaping Alexandria's urban character springs from the industrial boom of the late Victorian decades. What Renton hints at, Alexandria more manifestly retains: a consistent townscape of red sandstone two-storey flatted rows. Less trim and pervasive than once, it is this consistency of scale and material, set in a gridded mesh of streets, which enables the town to hold on to an urban identity which the depredations of roadworks and shopping centres have done their best to destroy.

Smollett Fountain

1 **Smollett Fountain**, 1870, Anderson & MacLeod
Commemorating the philanthropy of Alexander Smollett, *a kind and just landlord* and local MP, the fountain monumentalises the centre of

town in the form of a tiered Mercat Cross. It rises in three stages each enhanced by ornate convex parapets supported on massive shafts of silver and pink granite.

Opposite the fountain, **93-102 Main Street**, 1895, has a decorative red ashlar façade, busy with stepping string-coursing, pediments and chimneys. Taller and more assured is the **Royal Bank of Scotland**, **127-133** Main Street, 1891, Peddie & Kinnear, a symmetrical palace, its balustraded cornice interrupted by grandly pedimented dormers.

Older two-storey sandstone buildings still define stretches of Main Street, shops and flats marching gable-to-gable though not without interruption and intervention. **McKenzie's Bar**, **39-43** Main Street, 1852, uses a scrolled chimney to effect central emphasis. Less shabby, **Lea Park**, **274** Main Street, and **Southend Cottage**, **280** Main Street – the latter marred by an inappropriate dormer – preserve a more detached elegance from early Victorian days. **Rowantreebank House**, **294** Main Street, *c.*1820, older and austere, holds hard to the street-line. Recent shopping infill,

2 by contrast, is banal. At **Smollett Street** there is still a delightful rear lane from which the ubiquitous outside stairs give access to first-floor flats.

3 Four-in-a-block housing in **Queen's Drive** and **Wylie Avenue** by Joseph Weekes is built in rough-faced red sandstone, while the cottage villas of **Middleton Street**, 1882, and the mansions of **Upper Smollett Street** and **Main Street** are generally in red ashlar. Of these last, the Jacobean façade of **Belleville** at the north end of town and **St Ann's**, *c.*1880, in the south, its round-arched windows and fretwork reminiscent of early Alexander Thomson, are noteworthy.

4 **Bridge Street Church**, 1908, David Barclay The most flamboyant of Alexandria's churches sits obliquely to the street grid corner, entered through a castellated porch above which cusped pinnacles and flying buttresses create a complexity of forms heightened by the rough red stone. Transepts are doubled, stair units are curved, ornament is lavish: altogether an extravagant show in Late Decorated Gothic.

By comparison **St Mungo's Episcopal Church**, 1894-5, J M Crawford, on **Queen's Drive**, is modest, all in simple pointed idiom. Alone on **Albert Street**, the **Methodist**

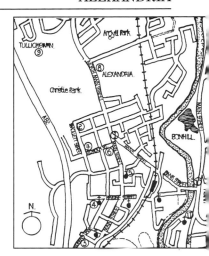

Below *Smollett Street.*
Bottom *Belleville*

Top *St Andrew's Parish Church.*
Above *Ewing Gilmour Institute*

Church, 1877-8, Malcolm Stark, is plain fare too. Equally isolated and plain, but more severely dignified, is the **Baptist Church**, 1897, formerly Bridge Street U P Church, a hall kirk with a pedimented Georgian front.

5 **St Andrew's Parish Church**, 1840
A painted stone nave of tall round-arched windows, its streetfront gable has an inset steeple so squat as to suggest the omission of some intermediate stage. Clock façades, gables and pinnacles around the neck of the spire serve only to draw attention to hunched ungainliness. Nonetheless, sited in the slow curve of Main Street, the steeple works well in the street scene.

6 **Ewing Gilmour Institute**, 1881-4,
Robert Thomson
Built to foster the *mental recreation and moral improvement* of the young men of the Vale, the Institute now serves as the local library. The pink ashlar façade to Gilmour Street is a brilliantly calculated composition of temple front, pediments and windows differing in size but sharing a proportional resonance. Formal devices drawn from Alexander Thomson are everywhere evident. Rear extensions, 1927, defer weakly to the lines of the original building.

Conditions for the girls in the dyeing works of the Vale were notorious. As late as 1911 John Gray of Grange Place, Alexandria, recorded a damning deposition during an enquiry into the working environment at Levenbank Works: *The work done is mixing aniline black. The fumes are poisonous. After working three or four hours in the place the girls become ashen grey, their lips and ears blue, and their cheeks yellow. I have seen women faint on account of the fumes ... The paper in which the girls bring their lunch turns quite yellow ... Scarcely any of the Vale of Leven girls will work in this department now. They get girls from outside the district who do not know what the work means.*

7 **Masonic Temple**, 1888-91, J A Campbell
William Ewing Gilmour put up the money for this Institute for Working Girls built at the opposite end of Gilmour Street. Tough and muscularly Scottish, a combination of Baronial keep and Renaissance halls forms a protective L-plan around the softer anglicised Arts & Crafts of the rear. All more masonic than maidenly.

Masonic Temple

8 **Argyll Motor Works**, 1905-6, Halley & Neil
The most extraordinary industrial palace in
Scotland. Suddenly, at the north end of Main
Street, it appears on the right: a 540 ft façade
of red sandstone dominated by a baroque
towered centrepiece crowned by a copper-
covered egg. Once, when car output here was
the highest in Europe, the dome was gilded and
*glittered like a fallen star when the sun struck
it*. Now that depression has struck, prospects
are gloomy. But the architecture remains; a
redundant cathedral of work void of sanctuary
and a reproachful reminder of the prosperity
the men of the Vale once made possible.

Argyll Motor Works

Opposite is **Christie Park**, entered past the
loggia of a Baronial **lodge**, 1902, by James
Miller. A little to the north are the curved walls
at the gates of the estate of Robert Lugar's
Tullichewan Castle, *c.*1808, demolished
1954. Here the **lodge**, early 19th century, is in
castellated Tudor Gothic, as indeed was
Tullichewan.

Below *Tullichewan Castle.*
Bottom *Vale of Leven Hospital*

9 Next comes **Vale of Leven Hospital**, 1957,
Joseph Gleave. It has grown erratically over
the years but the close-packed mullions and
cedar boarding of the ward blocks still exert
some uniformity of rhythm and material.
Downhill is **Vale of Leven Swimming Pool**,
1973, by Blair & McWiggan, brown brick walls
stretched out beneath a black mansard roof.

On the eastern side of town everything is in
turmoil. A new **shopping centre**, 1976, leads
nowhere; new roads confuse. Since the
demolitions of 1973, **Bank Street** – formerly
Ferry Loan – has lost all coherence: only the

Dumbarton District Libraries

Gillanders & Mack Photography

Bonhill Bridge

Keith/Brown

balustraded portico and flanking portals of the **Public Hall**, 1862, for long the Hall Cinema, have anything like the architectural dignity needed for Alexandria's eastern approaches. Opposite the portico, is the bowstring **Bonhill Bridge**, 1898, Crouch & Hogg; built to supersede the infamous *Bawbee Brig*, 1836, designed by the Glasgow engineer C Atherton, it, too, has been superseded by a new **bow suspension structure**, 1987, by Strathclyde Regional Council Roads Department Engineers.

10

VALE OF LEVEN: East
Industrial Estate

A graceful pedimented portico, set against a plain ashlar wall incised with the words VALE OF LEVEN INDUSTRIAL ESTATE is hardly the most high-tech portal. Towering above the trees to dominate the Leven valley for miles around is the immense bulk of the **Hiram Walker Whisky Blending Plant**, 1977. Beyond lie 1950s red brick factories; symmetrically stressed offices and saw-tooth roofs are typical.

Strathleven House, *c.*1690

One of Scotland's most valuable country houses, a seven-bay hip-roofed mansion built for William Cochrane of Kilmaronock, perhaps to the design of James Smith or Alexander McGill. There is a rude vigour in the pediment of the south front, in the hefty quoining and in the abstemious advancing mass of two wide wings linked to the main house by screen walls.

Strathleven House

Dumbarton District Libraries

A Doric T-plan porch was added c.1860. For years the property has been deserted and defiled and, though some panelling and plasterwork have been saved, the condition of the fabric is perilously close to national disaster. Nonetheless, thanks to the work of the Scottish Historic Buildings Trust, a rescue operation is at last under way: Strathleven House may yet re-emerge as a Business Training College, a fitting renewal in its industrial estate context.

Hidden in the trees nearby is a **doocot**, early 18th century, a two-storey square structure pedimented on the north and south. The upper chamber, containing stone nesting boxes, sits on a vaulted ground floor.

BONHILL

Over the hill from Strathleven House lies Bonhill, originally a medieval settlement on the old droving route from Argyll at the crossing of the Leven and, as its Gaelic name implies, *at the foot of the burn*. But, just as the burn has vanished – culverted in 1929 – so most of the old village has gone too and the place is now most strongly perceived as row upon row of council housing terraces contoured up the slopes of the valley. There is some sense of community focus at **Ladyton Centre** but only the orange brick and monopitch roofs of **St Ronan's Primary School**, 1975, Boys Jarvis Partnership, afford relief from the white-walled monotony of it all.

Consistency, not monotony, was the pattern of the older, lower, village which housed the local printers and dyers. The only red rows to survive are those along **Union Street**, c.1880, and at **1-43 Dillichip Terrace**, 1885, an austere flatted terrace with outside stairs and outhouses tidily organised along a rear lane. At **472** and **478 Main Street**, c.1830, the more elegant legacy of an earlier generation clings to life.

11 **Bonhill Parish Church**, 1836, John Baird
This is the oldest parish in the Vale, recorded as early as the 14th century. During the 18th century two churches were erected, one in 1747, another c.1797, trouble with the foundations of the latter necessitating the building of the present structure. The style is muted Perpendicular with a castellated tower over the porch. In the kirkyard are several 18th-century stones, a tomb, 1826, erected in memory of a local Covenanter, Robert Nairn,

The Argyll drovers found themselves subject to an impost or customs levy exercised by the garrison at Dumbarton Castle. In the 17th century the burgh of Dumbarton was also given a legal right to claim a toll on *ilk cow, ox, horse or stot*. Repeated attempts to evade these taxes were made but, by stationing soldiers at Bonhill where the cattle crossed the Leven, the Castle could ensure effective control of passage. In 1664 six drovers brought an action against Lord Blantyre, the Duke of Lennox's tacksman, and against the ferryman *at the Boat of Bonhill* accusing them of the *spulzie*, i.e. illegal seizure, of their beasts. The case was finally settled in 1673 in favour of the drovers, largely on the grounds of *there being another custom due to the town of Dumbarton*.

Bonhill Parish Church

who died for his faith in 1685, and, around the perimeter, a succession of mausoleums built by the heritors, some 18th century and one, 1870, constructed by the Martins of Auchendennan as a low buttressed Romanesque arch under a stone-slated roof.

Dalmonach School *c.*1835
Built with paternalistic zeal for the *half-timer* pupils from Dalmonach Works, schoolroom and schoolhouse sit by the riverside at the works gates close to the bridge across to Alexandria. Here, too, were housed the Mechanics Institute & Library, and, as the pointed arches seem to imply, one of the earliest Sunday Schools in the Vale.

JAMESTOWN
Developed from the hamlet of Damhead, situated close to the Dam of Balloch which drove the local meal mill, Jamestown was the creation of the Orr Ewing family who began Turkey-red dyeing and printing here in 1845.

Late Victorian admiration for what was described as *in all respects a model village* seems hard to believe for, with the demise of Levenbank Print Works, Jamestown has died. The few buildings remaining are as one might expect: some rubble cottages, plain with dressed stone margins. The **Locheil Bar** and **Bellvue**, *c.*1830, gabled late Georgian houses, again severely plain but each with a Roman Doric doorpiece. A little unusual, however, is a narrow-fronted shop and flat at **222-224 Main Street**, 1892, the single canted bay in its gable façade splayed out from a faceted fascia below.

Top *222-224 Main Street*. Above *Jamestown Parish Church*

2 **Jamestown Parish Church**, 1869-70, Clarke & Bell
Although otherwise plain pointed, the church has two fine assets: a large four-light nave gable window with wheel tracery and, to the left, a tall spire rising above the high pinnacled buttresses of a belfried steeple.

BALLOCH
Balloch's origins are medieval. At the south of Loch Lomond, which cuts a deep gash 23 miles up into the Highlands, the moated site of **Balloch Castle**, 1238-1390, once a stronghold of the Earls of Lennox, can still be detected. Centuries later, when mountain and flood drew romantically inclined travellers north, the beauty of the location and the opportunities for tourism which it offered became apparent.

Dumbarton District Libraries

Balloch Castle

As early as 1817 there were steamer excursions on the Loch aboard the *Marion*. In 1841-2 a toll suspension bridge was built to cross the Leven where the old Ferry House Inn stood on the east bank. **Balloch Hotel** is still there, a black-and-white concoction of old and not-so-old building. In 1850 the railway arrived to ensure the village's future. Today, the steamer still sails, the tourists come by train, bus and car, and the Leven is full of small craft – a bright riverside scene worlds away from the industrial wasteland that begins only yards downstream.

From the old bridge at Balloch Hotel, now a lattice-beam structure of 1908, to the **Lomond Road Bridge**, 1934, several large houses have taken advantage of riparian sites. On the west
3 bank is the **Tullichewan Hotel**, 1893, a large Arts & Crafts style villa with half-timbered bracketed bayed gables, red brick chimneys, tile-hung walls and a big English roof. To the
4 south, off Lomond Road, sits **Fisherwood**, *c.*1910, equally English and picturesque.

5 **Riverside Motor Inn**, *c.*1825
Built on the east bank of Lennoxbank by John Stuart, the proprietor of Levenbank Works, Jamestown, this distinctive Georgian mansion has been all but swamped by later commercialism. Now abandoned, like so much in the Vale, its stylistic quirkiness – medieval elements set in a classical country house mould – can still be enjoyed; between corner bartizans a battlemented parapet rises in pediment form above a pointed arch entry.

Below *River Leven at Balloch*.
Middle *Tullichewan Hotel*.
Bottom *Riverside Motor Inn*

Sinclair

Sinclair

Sinclair

Top *The Cottage.*
Above *Boturich Castle*

Balloch's setting at the foot of Loch Lomond is one of great beauty, all the more attractive after the jaded industrial landscape of the Vale of Leven. Its Celtic name, *Bealach*, has the fittingly poetic translation, *pass to the field of smooth waters.*

In **Drymen Road** – an attractive, suddenly suburban, tree-lined avenue – is **Roselea**, 1888, distinguished by decorative bargeboards and segmental lintels to its ground-floor windows. Outstanding, however, are **Warwick**
6 **House** and **The Cottage**, *c*.1930, both mansarded cottage villas with charming porches, canted bays and swept dormers.

7 **Balloch Castle**, 1808-9, Robert Lugar
John Buchanan of Ardoch, an original partner in the Glasgow Ship Bank, commissioned this castellated mansion from the London architect Lugar; with Tullichewan and Boturich it was one of three such projects Lugar carried out in Dunbartonshire – designs which, when published in 1811, became highly influential on the development of the secular Gothic Revival. A free symmetrical composition, battlemented and turreted – *a very good specimen of the Castle-Gothic* – Balloch swallows up an earlier plainer building. The principal façade has an unusually slow concave curve ending in a bellcoted clock tower, 1830, over the services wing. Castle, garden and estate are today part of a beautiful 200-acre Country Park which stretches along the south-east shore of Loch Lomond. In the Castle, Page & Park have designed a crisp **Interpretative Centre**, 1986.

8 **Boturich Castle**, from 1830, Robert Lugar
Boturich, another of the homes of John Buchanan of Ardoch, sits above the loch about a mile north of Balloch Castle. Lugar's rebuilding, *c*.1830, of the 15th-century castle scarcely imparts a satisfactory unity, though it must be likely his intentions were never wholly realised. Yet, there are picturesque corners. Scott, Stephen & Gale had a hand in matters, too, in 1834, while the octagonal entrance tower was not added until 1850.

GARTOCHARN & KILMARONOCK
The road to Drymen (see *Stirling & the Trossachs* in this series) runs north from Balloch. To the left is **Ashfield House**, 1844, a small Georgian-style mansion quite plain but for its pedimented pilastered doorpiece.

Westerton House, *c*.1810
Seen through the trees across its lawn, Westerton is an elegant house with pilastered quoins, porthole motifs and urn-capped pediment. Closer to, however, there is a tell-

tale heaviness to the mouldings betraying substantial recasting. While the Georgian residence may have grown from humbler origins it has been much altered and added to, c.1909. Nonetheless, it maintains sturdy dignity and preserves the elevational rump of a Gothick chapel.

At Gartocharn, some cottages, rubble-built in local red sandstone, may date from the late 18th century but the growth of the hamlet came later. There is an inn, once known from the nickname of its proprietrix as *Old Lucky's* but now, trim and smartly painted, rather refined as **Gartocharn Hotel**. There is a stone-porched former school 1876, extended c.1901, surviving as an **art gallery**.

Between Ashfield House and Westerton House is a farm named Old Kirk, while nearby is another called The Shannacles, a corruption of the Gaelic *Sean eaglais*, which also means *old church*. All of this points to some ancient religious foundations perhaps instituted by the sixth-century St Kessog evangelising from his monastery on Inchtavannach in Loch Lomond, or by St Ronan in the eighth century, since it was he who gave his name to the parish of Kilmaronock. But, though Bronze Age burial cists have been unearthed nearby, there is now no sign of a church.

Kilmaronock Church, 1813
Built to replace an earlier, possibly medieval, church that had *much the appearance of antiquity* and by 1811 had fallen into *a very bad and ruinous condition*, this simple kirk in rust-red stone has a stout classical dignity. The entrance is austerely set in ashlar below a pedimented gable while inside, below a plaster vault, the hall is lit by tall round-arch windows. No steeple here but a bulbously domed little belfry sitting squatly on the ridge.

Kilmaronock Castle, 14th century
Some half-mile north of the church is a massive but dangerously ruined tower held together by centuries-old ivy. Half a vaulted basement and another vast vault above a vanished second floor remain. In the rent-rubble walls, random openings and gunloops abound. Above an arched window the Dennistoun arms may indicate 14th-century origins.

Kilmaronock Church

Kilmaronock House and Castle

Dwarfed by the castle **Kilmaronock House**, 1901, affects a false but endearing Baronial grandeur: ogee-domed stair tower, crow-step gables, double-height transom-and-mullion glazing, and here and there a faint flavour of Arts & Crafts. A similar predilection for Baronialising crops up at **Auchenlarich**, 1894, a farmhouse on the Croftamie road south of Gartocharn earnestly transformed by turrets, crow-stepping and a solidly buttressed porch.

ABER

North of Gartocharn, closer to the Loch and the mouth of the Endrick, is the lost village of **Aber**, where *bonnet lairds* held small plots but enjoyed unusual rights of pasturage and fishing. Originally tenant farmers of William Cochrane of Kilmaronock Castle, they suffered so frequently from the Strathendrick raids of Rob Roy MacGregor and his reivers (see *Stirling & the Trossachs* in this series) that Cochrane gladly got rid of his feudal obligations by allowing them to buy their own lands however small – an exceptional privilege. There are traces of the old settlement, including the crumbling walls of **Aber Mill**, where a lintel stone is cut with the inscription *JOHN GALBRAITH 1806*, and a few cottages nestling haphazardly in this lovely spot.

Ross Priory: plasterwork

Ross Priory, 1810-16, J Gillespie Graham
The original seat of the Buchanans of Ross, 14th century, was rebuilt in 1695 and then remodelled in 1810. The wings of the 17th-century house were removed and the accommodation enlarged to the north and east within a symmetrical yet strongly Gothic skin.

Ross Priory

RIAS Collection

Below *Hamilton House*. Middle
Cameron House. Bottom *Porch,
Auchendennan House*

There are tall doubled and tripled lancets, a
three-arch buttressed porch above a flying
stair, and crocketed pinnacles accenting the
skyline. The house is now owned by the
University of Strathclyde.

LOCH LOMOND: South

Past **Hamilton House**, formerly Woodbank, late
18th century – an impressive five-bay pedimented
mansion with a hipped and chimneyed roof – the
old Loch Lomond road north out of Balloch now
comes to an inexplicable dead end. The lochside
must be reached from the new road marginally to
the west.

RCAHMS

Cameron House, *c.*1830 and 1865,
William Spence
Baronialised with a tall asymmetrical tower by
Spence; despite a liberal bombardment with
bartizans, hefty dormers and string-courses,
the lower Georgian house of 1830 is still
evident. Now lavishly appointed as a leisure
centre and hotel at the foot of the loch, but still
recognisably a country house. The setting, *well
sheltered and commanding a fine view of the
watery expanse*, is magnificent.

Dumbarton District Libraries

Auchendennan House, 1864-6, John Burnet
On the A82, just past the **Mid Lodge**, *c.*1850,
entry to Cameron House estate, this must be
Scotland's grandest youth hostel. Built as a rich
man's castle, every Baronial device has been
deployed in hard-edged mechanical panoply. The
Mannerist aberrations of a colossal *porte cochère*,
added by A N Paterson in 1902, anticipate the
richly decorative interiors. There is a fine
conservatory to the west.

RCAHMS

Lomond Castle Hotel, 1865,
Campbell Douglas & Stevenson
Formerly Auchenheglish House, this lochside hotel (now roofless) has a softer Baronial aspect. The entrance front is wide and low and wholly domestic, but from the stumpy-columned arched porch the roofs build up almost imperceptibly towards the high ridges and turrets of the eastern side of the house.

Top Lomond Castle Hotel.
Above Arden House

Arden House, 1868, John Burnet
Following his Baronial *tour de force* at Auchendennan, Burnet produced this equally vigorous design for Sir James Lumsden, then recently knighted Lord Provost of Glasgow. The roofscape is peppered with turrets – cones, pyramids and ogees – though the staircase turret of a six-storey central tower has gone. Burnet's porch is massive and bold, but lacks the bravura of Paterson's at Auchendennan.

In 1773, a few months after the completion of the new house, **Samuel Johnson** and **James Boswell** stopped over at Rossdhu during their celebrated *Tour of the Hebrides*. Lady Helen Colquhoun, justifiably proud of her new home found the good doctor's boorish manners insupportable. Discovering him drenched after boating in the Loch yet striding across her drawing room splashing water from his boots in all directions she is reported to have muttered *What a bear! Yes*, commented another guest, *he is no doubt a bear, but he is Ursus Major*, a remark doubtless as unbearable to Lady Helen as Johnson's behaviour.

Rossdhu House, 1772-4,
possibly Sir James Clerk
A short drive north of Arden the high arched portal of **Rossdhu South Lodge** is reached. Pairs of tall three-quarter columns support an entablature on which the painted arms of the Colquhouns of Luss are raised on the skyline. Behind the gates lies an estate rich in the built appurtenances of an ancient family. **Rossdhu Castle**, first referred to in a charter of 1541 as the *castle, tower and fortalice of Rosedew*, inhabited by the family until 1770, survives as a ruinous wall and, just north of the castle, the medieval **Chapel of St Mary**, dedicated 1469, used latterly as a burial ground, as little more.

Rossdhu House

The present **Rossdhu House**, 1772-4, erected by Sir James Colquhoun, 25th of Luss, is an Adam-style mansion built with stone quarried from the old castle. Adam may have been consulted, Sir James Clerk of Penicuik certainly was; but the executive hand belonged to John Baxter, who had worked with both

Glasgow Art Gallery and Museum

Adam and Clerk, while there is also evidence of payments to *Mr Thomas Brown, Architect at Renfrew*. There is a pedimented portico and a balustraded parapet; the portico and lower wings are of later date added by Sir James, 27th of Luss. The classical offices, which comprise **laundry**, **byre** and **coach house**, date from the early 19th century. A **sundial** in the walled garden south of the main house may, however, belong to the 17th century.

LUSS

The Colquhouns' **Estate Office**, sitting primly on a wooded rise beside the loch, is seen first. To the left are four estate cottages at **Low Aldochlay** sharing a rustic preference for grey-green random rubble walls and arched windows. At **High Aldochlay** appear two more cottages, steep-roofed with Gothic casements in metal.

The village grew around the church at the mouth of the Water of Luss. Records go back to the 13th century and in 1430 there is mention of a thatched church erected by the Bishop of Glasgow in memory of the local saint, St Kessog (see also *Stirling & the Trossachs* in this series). The present **Parish Church**, 1875, which was built to replace an *uncommonly good* one of 1771, is Gothic Revival, though it does use a medieval font and

Loch Lomond, painted by Horatio McCulloch, 1861

The Alpine scenery of Loch Lomond greatly appealed to Queen Victoria reminding her much of sails on Lake Lucerne. From the steamer, appropriately named *Prince Consort*, she sketched as best she could even though *it is most difficult to do so when the steamer keeps moving on.*

Below *Aldochlay*. Bottom *Kirk of Luss*

Sinclair

RCAHMS

53

Luss Parish Church

incorporates the **MacFarlane Stone**, 1612. There is a laird's loft for the Colquhouns and above the T-shaped plan a fine raftered roof, this same addiction to timber construction expressed in two delightful lich-gates. The walled graveyard contains two slabs from the seventh and eighth centuries and a rare Norse hogback stone of the 11th century.

When, towards the end of the 18th century, the Colquhoun estate began to develop slate quarrying and cotton spinning as well as agriculture, workers' cottages were built by the shingle beach close to the present pier. **Elmbank**, early 19th century, though not quite so favourably located, is typical and once served as the village inn. Around mid-century more cottages were built and it is these coursed rubble houses on **Pier Road**, with their piend roofs and diamond-latticed windows, which give Luss its architectural charm and consistency.

A narrow road climbs to **Edentaggart** through Glen Luss. The foundations of an ancient **chapel**, enclosed in 1852, can be found. Two small single-span bridges are also of interest: **Chapel Hill Bridge**, bearing the inscription *WILLIAM JOHN BUILT THIS BRIDGE 1777* and the **Ramshead Bridge**, so called because of the carving of a ram's head set into its rubble parapet to commemorate the fateful introduction of black-faced sheep at Glenmallochan Farm in 1749.

Top & above *Pier Road cottages.*
Below *Ben Lomond from Luss*

LOCH LOMOND: Islands

Off Luss is a cluster of little islands which add greatly to the beauty of the place whether seen from water or land. Closest to the shore are the islets of **Fraoch Eilaean**, to which the miscreant wives of Luss were committed, and **Inchtavannach**, *Island of the Monk's House*, where St Kessog established his monastery some

time in the sixth century. East of **Inchmoan**, where villagers used to cut their peat, is **Inchcruin** which once served as *an asylum for insane persons*. **Inchlonaig**, on the other hand, was reserved as the Colquhouns' deer-park; in 1839 it was inhabited by about 150 deer and *one family, who board persons that have been addicted to drink*. In earlier times the island's yew woods were carefully preserved for the manufacture of bows. On **Inchgalbraith** is a relic of the castle of the Galbraiths while at the west end of **Inchmurrin** an ancient fortalice of the Earls of Lennox dating from the 14th century is also in ruins. From Inchmurrin a string of seven islands, thought by Pennant to be the end of the Grampian chain of mountains, runs north-east towards Balmaha. Close to the east shore is **Inchcaillaich**, *Island of Nuns*, where beside the remains of a small chapel MacGregors lie buried.

LOCH LOMOND: North

The main road continues north from Luss giving spectacular views as the loch narrows below **Ben Lomond**. In such a setting the renovated trim of **Inverbeg Inn**, 1814, restored 1978 – shuttered windows and window boxes – looks almost Alpine.

Stuckgowan House, *c.*1820

The most beautiful house on the loch, Stuckgowan is that rare picturesque combination of Georgian taste and Gothic caprice. It is a charming house; a low hip-roofed cottage with pointed windows, hood mouldings and dormers symmetrically composed around a bow-fronted drawing room. Everything is delicate and graceful, from the attic lancets to a miniature elliptical gallery which lights the entrance hall. There is a lower wing on the north and a pavilion-roofed **North Lodge** with arched windows and latticed glazing.

In 1263 King Haakon of Norway sent a huge fleet around Kintyre into the Firth of Clyde. Running short of provisions off Rothesay he dispatched a force of galleys up Loch Long. At Arrochar the Norwegians pulled their vessels on rollers across the narrow neck of land to Tarbet on Loch Lomond, thereafter ravaging southwards through the Vale of Leven to the Firth. There is a Norse burial at Fruin Bridge which may date from this time.

In October of the same year, however, fierce gales threw the Norwegian fleet into confusion between the Cumbraes and the mainland helping the Scottish forces of Alexander III win the decisive Battle of Largs. Thereafter the Treaty of Perth (1266) assigned the Western Isles and the Isle of Man to the Scottish Crown.

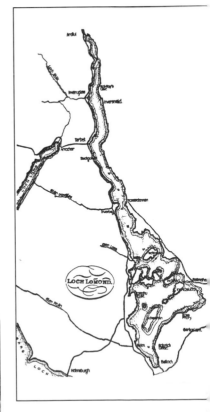

Stuckgowan House

TARBET

When Garnett reached Tarbet in 1798 he found *a decent looking inn*.today, the Italianate tower of **Edendarroch Hotel**, *c*.1855, can be glimpsed to the right, but the view is soon filled with the vast Baronial bulk of **Tarbet Hotel**, *c*.1850, 1878. Since the late 16th century there has been a coaching inn here, for it is only a short distance over the hill to Arrochar and Loch Long and the route west across the Rest-and-be-Thankful to Inveraray. Here, too, the railway from Glasgow, having swept around the Gareloch and Loch Long from Helensburgh cuts back to follow the western bank of Loch Lomond to the north.

Below *Tarbet Hotel.* Middle *Tarbet Tea Room.* Bottom *Craigenarden Viaduct*

Tarbet is a quiet sleepy little place: some older estate cottages, a good group of stone-built dormered cottages built for Loch Sloy's hydro-electric workers at **Ballyhennan Crescent**, *c*.1950. A neat gable-fronted **tea-room** and **Post Office**, early 19th century, with its neighbour **Lochview**, early 19th century, a severe twin-doored Georgian house, form a roadside courtyard that is evidently a centre of village life.

The A82 winds on, clinging to the lochside. At **Inveruglas** a pleasant courtyard farm catches the eye. Then comes the massive pilastered box of **Sloy Power Station**, 1950. Before Ardlui, at **Craigenarden Viaduct**, 1891, the railway makes its impact tower beside the roadway, an arcade of eight arches on rough-faced piers supporting a castellated parapet to the permanent way. For those walking the West Highland Way the place to stop is further north beyond the end of the loch. **Inverarnan Drovers' Inn**, early 18th century, is old – established 1705, says the swinging inn sign – rough-rubble walled with gabled dormers and porch, and full of the smell of wood smoke from a warming bar-room fire. Beyond, through Glen Falloch, lies Crianlarich and the north.

Inverarnan Drovers' Inn

ARDOCH

The estate stretched west from Dumbarton to the
outskirts of Cardross, keeping march with the
shoreline and the increasing width of the Clyde.
Where the old ferry house of **Clydebank Farm**
sits out its retirement (its twin facing on the
opposite bank), a Renfrew lawyer built **Cats
Castle** in 1888, its handsome Scots Baronial
façades festooned with feline forms. **Ardoch
House**, *c.*1780, a lovely colonial-style cottage with
splayed flanking wings at the foot of **Lee Brae**, is
now fronted by a low square entrance tower with
pyramidal roof. Beautiful elliptical drawing room
hung with family portraits. **Ardochmore Farm**
marks the site of the ancient castle of the Bontine
family, whose descendants through marriage –
the Grahams of Gartmore – built Ardoch.

CARDROSS

In 1852 no more than a handful of cottages
clustered around kirk, inn and mill at the
crossing of Auchenfroe Burn by Craigend; half
a mile or so to the west, Geilston with its burn
and mill was even smaller. Once the railway
from Dumbarton arrived and connected with
the line from Helensburgh in 1857, a station
was built between the two streams and
Cardross expanded.

Kilmahew Chapel, from 15th century
The kirk served as a Protestant *chapel of ease*
in the 17th century from which part of the east
end may date. Reconstructed 1953-5, by Ian
Lindsay & Partners, as a single-storey
roughcast cottage with a slightly higher crow-
step gabled east end with roll-moulded and
chamfered window jambs and a small red
sandstone bellcote added by Lindsay at the
west. Early Christian standing stone in the
vestibule (*below*).

Top *Cats Castle.*
Above *Ardoch House*

Built by **Robert Graham of
Gartmore** who returned to
Scotland after 18 years in
Jamaica, Ardoch's most famous
occupant was also a descendant
of the Bontines. Robert Bontine
Cunninghame Graham (1852-
1936) became the first
President of the Scottish
Labour Party on its foundation
in 1888. He had achieved
notoriety the previous year by
leading a demonstration to
Trafalgar Square in support of
the public's right to
demonstrate there without
police permission. While
Cunninghame Graham's urge
to travel ended his career in
politics and led him to Spain,
Morocco and Argentina and a
second, more successful career
as a writer, his nationalistic
pride was strong, and he agreed
to become President of the
National Party of Scotland
when it was formed in 1928.
Selling the family home,
Gartmore House, he finally
confirmed his ancestral links
with Dumbarton, returning to
Ardoch, his *small house on the
side of the Clyde.*

Above Old Parish Church.
Right Shield and carved detail

Old Parish Church,
1826-7, James Dempster
The first church on the site was
erected in 1643-4 after the
parish boundaries had been
redrawn, and the centre of the
Parish removed from
Levengrove Park, Dumbarton.
In 1826 a second church was
commissioned. A battlemented
and long-pinnacled tower with
its bracing gable, each
diagonally buttressed, are all
that remain of Dempster's
Perpendicular Gothic. Bombed
in 1941, the church was later
razed, 1954, to an elevated
lawn set at sill height, a
commemorative strategy that
has proved wholly successful.
More personal memorials are
gathered in its shadow,
including two identical
mausoleum enclosures (*right*),
castellated and gunlooped, on
the western margin of the
burial plot.

Kilmahew Castle, 15th and 17th century,
half a mile east of Kirkton, the ancient seat of
the Napiers until 1820. Thereafter much
rebuilt in an attempt to turn it into a Gothick
mansion. Never complete, now ruinous; the
high rubble walls affording shelter to local
owls.

The eastern end of the village preserves some
early black-and-white gabled houses: the
White House, part 18th century, formerly
Bainfield House, on the corner of Carman
Road, **Bainfield**, *c.*1810, an old single-storey
ferry house and one-time inn; **Burnside
Cottage**, late 18th century (?), with new slated
roof and piended porch; **Cardross Inn**, part
18th century, expanded repeatedly from its
farmhouse origins.

Moore's Bridge (*left*) crossing the Auchenfroe
Burn, still bears an original coat of arms stone,
dated 1688, and an inscription NOT WE BUT GOD
over the name of its benefactress Jean Moore
née Watson. Largely a Victorian restoration
with dressed red sandstone framing the grey
remnants of older construction.

Bloomhill House, *c*.1838, bayed and gabled
with modest Jacobean pretension, replaced an
earlier mansion of *c*.1775, the stable yard of
which can be reached through a pedimented
pend off Carman Road. **Shira Lodge**, red
sandstone, is distinguished less for its
Jacobean gable than for the violently reversed
entasis on its porch columns. Ochre sandstone
is adopted at **Ardenvohr**, 1885, and **Seafield**,
1885, two large bayed Victorian villas off Peel
Street similarly distinguished by an enormous
cavetto cornice. North are the fairways of
Cardross Golf Club; the **Clubhouse**, 1956, has
all the hallmarks of 1930s modernism – white
walls, flat roofs, curving glazed lounges,
porthole windows.

Below *Golf Clubhouse.*
Bottom *Rural seat*

Station Road cuts south to the railway.
Opposite A N Paterson's **Rural Seat**, 1932, is
Villafield, *c*.1890, Cardross's only tenement.
Beyond are **Marand**, *c*.1905, pavilion roofed
with a roughcast upper storey jutting boldly
from red brick walls below, and the half-
timbered **Dana Cottage**, *c*.1900, once the Post
Office. Down **Church Avenue** is a short series
of red sandstone houses, *c*.1875, made
pleasantly complex by piended dormers and
bowed roofs.

Cardross Parish Church, 1871-2,
John Burnet
Built as a Free Church, it became the parish
kirk in the early 1950s after the wartime
destruction of Dempster's church (see p.58) at
Craigend. Marking the entrance on **Church
Avenue** is a straight-edged belfry tower

Parish Church

capped by a stone pyramid behind which the nave roof dips low over deep flanking buttresses. Severe Gothic is relieved by Decorated tracery in the main gable, a telephone-dial rose in the transept but especially by the soft texture of rubble walls. The iron **gates** on Station Road are magnificent; so, too, some of the sections of Hannah Frew Paterson's embroidered panels, 1981, hanging inside.

Broomfield and **Laigh Barrs**, *c*.1830, are plain, skew-gabled, flatted dwellings. Past Reay Avenue, **Fruin** and **Finlas**, *c*.1855, in polychromatic sandstone, are similar, the latter with a porthole through its central chimneyed gable. The **Castle Hotel**, *c*.1885, built as Beatrice Villa, is symmetrical Tudor with the lop-sided addition of an attractive conservatory dining room.

Right *Geilston Halls*. Below *St Peter's College*

Geilston Halls, 1889-90, Honeyman & Keppie, stand back from the road: the style is castellated Gothic, the halls entered through gabled arched portals and guarded by a battlemented tower on the western gable. **Woodneuk**, *c*.1830, opposite, is painted rubble with neat gabled and pilastered dormers and an unflattering glazed porch.

Auchenfroe House, *c*.1815
A central semi-octagonal projection with a tripartite window at first floor and a pedimented columned porch below adds unorthodox distinction to the late Georgian model.

Kilmahew House, 1865-8, John Burnet
Built for John William Burns, son of the founder of the Cunard Line, it is thoroughly Baronial, though not Burnet's best. All the usual Scottish elements are employed, plus some unexpected Star of David tracery in two tall staircase windows.

Studio Brett

St Peter's College, 1958-66,
Gillespie Kidd & Coia
The wonder of a visit to Kilmahew estate; a
tour de force of spatial brilliance inside and out.
In the long main block a step storeyed cross
section of study cells builds up over refectory
and chapel while a jutting library wing soars
out spectacularly over the trees of the valley
below. The proxy of Le Corbusier is
marvellously validated, though the passage of
time has wrought a cruelly undeserved fate.
After only ten years the seminary closed and
since 1976 efforts to find a future for the
award-winning building have so far failed.

St Peter's College

Drumhead
Opposite Kilmahew Chapel a long drive leads
past a timber-porched **lodge** at Geilston Burn
to reach this Victorian Baronial casing of an
earlier house. Decidedly vertical in emphasis it
is a composition of tall three-storey elements
with elongated window proportions, steep crow-
step gables and, highest of all, a cylindrical
stair tower with candle-snuffer roof.

Below *Drumhead.*
Bottom *Darleith House*

Dumbarton District Libraries

Darleith House, from 17th century
The seat of the Yuille family, a ruinous
Georgian mansion with pedimented centrepiece and flat-topped porch of coupled Ionic
columns situated on the edge of the moor; an
earlier fortalice has disappeared, while later
additions disrupt the neoclassical composure of
the main house. Nearby are a ruined chapel

Dick

61

Above *Doocot, Darleith.*
Right *Geilston House*

and a powerfully architectonic **doocot**, *c.*1790, in which triangular and rectangular prisms combine splendidly with cylinder and cone: off the beaten track but not to be missed.

Geilston House, from 1766
Two mortars, said to have been used at Corunna, stand fast on the lawn in front of the picturesque L-shaped range of Geilston. The development of the house spans several centuries, although evidence of this is well disguised. Principally two-storey, the exterior is unified by crow-stepped gables and harled walls. There is a restored **stables** block and a square 18th-century **doocot** with hipped roof and a triangular stone pigeon entrance. Behind the house lies a magnificent **walled garden**.

Longbarn

The farm road opposite leads to **Longbarn**, 1932, built for William Denny in much the manner suggested by its name. The thatched roof has gone, reputedly burnt by a spark from a passing steam locomotive, but the replacement slate still swells at the eaves in convincing fashion. One-room deep the house is an attractive, if geographically inappropriate, example of 1930s Tudor-style design. Close by is the ancient cottage of **Rosebank** where the novelist A J Cronin was born.

Following the railway towards Helensburgh the mansion of **Moore Park**, 1864, is soon reached; notable not so much for the original villa as for the 1892 extension built by the Glasgow Procurator-Fiscal and writer, David Murray. Half-timbered, with a coy griffin overlooking the entrance, the house has a great battlemented bastion of a tower on the south-west corner.

Mollandhu Farmhouse, 1946, Joseph Weekes
The courtyard range behind is original, but the
black-and-white farmhouse was built to replace
an earlier cottage bombed in March 1941
during German raids on Clydeside. Flat-roofed
with a striated entrance arch and a boldly
protruding bow window, the design is a
departure for its architect, but still with the
inherent Scottishness by which his work can be
recognised.

Mollandhu Farmhouse

Cardross Crematorium, 1960,
Watson, Salmond and Gray
Shallow, copper-clad roofs betray the
Scandinavian influences in this stylish
crematorium-cum-cemetery complex. A red
rosemary-tiled cottage guards the gateway, the
building itself providing a second, momentary
barrier in the form of an arched entrance tower
with pyramidal roof. Beyond, a loggia supported
on deep stone pilasters has a striking winged
sculpture in stone by Hew Lorimer inside.

Below *Cardross Crematorium*.
Bottom *Ardmore House*

ARDMORE
Linked to Cardross parish and managed as a
nature reserve by the Scottish Wildlife Trust,
Ardmore was very likely once an island; a mass
of quartz-studded puddingstone rock thrusting
into the Firth of Clyde. There was a laird's
house on the **Hill of Ardmore** as far back as
1654 and the present mansion, 1806,
encompasses a plain, but substantial earlier
building in Regency garb – a battlemented
central tower with segmental window (blind in
part) raised above simple, stuccoed wings.
Impressive for its dignified presence on the
outward slope of the promontory.

Keppoch House

Ardmore was laid out towards the end of the 18th century by General Thomas Geils. Interesting are three towers which may date from the 16th or 17th century; two are located close to the cliff-face south of the mansion house, one over 30 ft high with loop holes and windows, the other perched directly above and complete with the original conical roof on centre post. Behind the house are the splendid remains of a telescopic lookout tower – three concentric circles, the inner two of local stone, the central portion still housing a spiral stair.

MacKinlay

Keppoch House, 1820
Past the buttressed perimeter of the 1816 walled garden and hidden, for the most part, among blossom and bluebells; a chaste pavilion block erected on the site of an old peel tower. Elegant pedimented centrepiece, at the foot of which rises a pillared porch sheltering a curving glazed entrance screen. The dining room walls are lined with 18th-century timber panelling removed from St Anne's Church, Belfast.

COLGRAIN
The former **East Lodge** of Camis Eskan house crouches in the shadow of a magnificent beech hedge. Stone built and pleasantly proportioned, it provides clues to the style of the house, but offers little invitation to investigate further. As Helensburgh encroaches, farmland gives way to suburbia and with the depressing spectacle of **Hermitage Academy**, 1966, Baron Bercott & Associates, destroys the scale and effect of Camis Eskan's Georgian **West Lodge**, 1840, probably David Hamilton, an attractive little building with pillared porchway and acorn-fashioned finials.

Drumfork House, 1748
Predating Helensburgh itself, a studious, two-storey house with few architectural pretensions, lying on the ancient drove road from Loch Lomondside to Drumfork Ferry, where cattle were shipped to Greenock.

Drumfork House

Dumbarton District Libraries

Camis Eskan, from 1648
Much remodelled, 1840 by David Hamilton, and 1915 by A N Paterson, the house belonged for 500 years to the Dennistoun family who, in 1836, transferred ownership to Colin Campbell of Breadalbane. Briefly a tuberculosis sanatorium and geriatric hospital, the house

Camis Eskan

retains a fine interior and has found new life as luxury apartments. Paterson's broad bay windows, with Gibbs surrounds, ironwork and urns ensure a Georgian flavour. South is a splendid, albeit ruinous, octagonal two-storey **doocot** (late 17th century) while north is the **Home Farm**, with its lofty courtyard archway.

CRAIGENDORAN, from 1877

Craigendoran has its origins in the abortive *station on the sea* scheme conceived by the North British Railway Company owing to Helensburgh Pier's lack of proper coaling facilities and its distance from the existing railway station. The company, aware of the debilitating effect this was having on the service provided, moved to establish a new terminus on the sea-front. Howls of protest from local residents met these proposals; the genteel folk of this *flourishing and favourable watering-place* feared that a railway route along the waterfront would reduce Helensburgh to a *dirty coaling town*. Thwarted, but undaunted, the railway company sought parliamentary approval to realise their scheme at nearby Craigendoran.

The terraced west side of **Craigendoran Avenue**, *c*.1900, represents the best of this small community. Solid two-storey houses with a spirited, seaside flavour are bedecked with jaunty gablets and oriels, bay windows and modestly decorative stonework and ironwork – terminating in the turreted corner of what was once the Lomond Hotel.

Craigendoran Pier was opened on 15 May 1882. Close by was a railway station with through platforms on the Helensburgh line and a bay platform, curving down to the pierhead. The pier was twin-armed, allowing four steamers to berth and was a considerable improvement on the quay at Helensburgh. Here, the North British Railway Company based their fleet, providing substantial competition for their south-bank based rivals, the Caledonian and Glasgow & South-Western Railway Companies. By the 1930s, however, Gourock and Wemyss Bay had become the most convenient railheads in the upper Firth and closure came in 1972.

Below *Craigendoran Avenue*. Bottom *PS Waverley at Craigendoran*

Helensburgh was named in honour of Lady Helen Sutherland, wife of Sir James Colquhoun, 8th Baronet of Colquhoun & Luss who, in 1752, bought the lands of Malig or Milligs on the north bank of the Clyde for £6500 from the daughter of Sir John Schaw of Greenock. His hope of establishing a rural settlement based on textile industries was not fulfilled. A feuing plan was commissioned from Charles Ross of Greenlaw, surveyor to the Luss Estates, yet it was not until 1803 that the grid-iron concept materialised in a survey of the town (now a Burgh of Barony) carried out by Peter Fleming of Glasgow.

Right *Town plan.*
Below *Railway poster*

HELENSBURGH
The town is deceptively homogeneous, a rigorous grid-iron layout of two-acre plots in which a disparate array of architectural styles co-exists, blurred by spectacular leafiness, yet reinforced by pronounced, regular contours from the backdrop of Glen Fruin to the sprawl of the Firth.

TOWN CENTRE
There is no town centre as such; the weekly markets and four annual fairs to which the burgh was originally entitled seem to have been staged well to the west of the present commercial core. At the junction of **Sinclair Street** and **Princes Street**, the purposeful regularity of Helensburgh's street pattern unfolds: definition coming first in the form of tenement and terrace, rapidly giving way to garden wall and hedgerow. A short stretch lined with tenements with ground floor shops opens up to reveal the waterfront and expansive panoramas of Greenock and Port Glasgow. To the immediate east and west is the modest commercial heart of the town, and in an area roughly two blocks deep by four blocks long, lies the town's pre-railway development, plotted on a density unmatched elsewhere in the locality.

Sinclair Street, c.1900

A **Municipal Buildings**, 1 East Princes Street,
1878, John Honeyman
On the site of the former Town Hall, scholarly
Scots Baronial, turreted and crow-stepped, the
Burgh Buildings make a handsome
cornerpiece: A N Paterson's 1906 addition,
originally comprising the Police Office and Fire
Station, is a freer, more modern interpretation
of the same Scots vocabulary, complete with
tall, chimneyed doocot to the rear and a
recumbent stone cat at second storey. The
Station Buildings, 1899, mark the western
terminus of the original Glasgow, Dumbarton
& Helensburgh Railway, a great glazed canopy
spanning effortlessly across the platforms.

*Left Municipal Buildings
extension. Below 40 Sinclair
Street. Bottom Old Parish
Church*

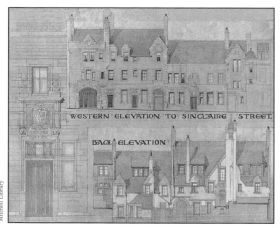

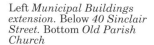

B **Former Conservative Association
Headquarters**, 40 Sinclair Street,
1894, Honeyman & Keppie
The sinuous flow of the stone parapet, the
elegant carving, and the extensive roof glazing
to the original top-floor billiard room all invite
speculation that Charles Rennie Mackintosh
may have contributed to this Glasgow Style
design. Muscular range of tenements alongside
by Frank Burnet & Boston, formerly the
Carlton Buildings, 1898.

C **Old Parish Church**, 4 East Clyde Street,
1846, Charles Wilson
Helensburgh's most prominent landmark,
visible – and vital – from land and sea, shorn of
church hall, nave, ancillary buildings and all
other dignities. The Italianate clock tower (to
which an eminently suitable porch was added
by Robert Wemyss in 1923) is now an
Information Centre.

67

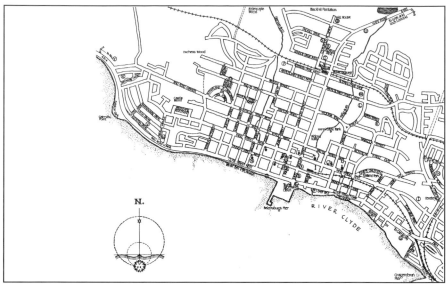

West Clyde Street

Despite the inadequacy of the pier, Helensburgh became accustomed to a daily steamer service linking the town with Glasgow and Greenock. By 1850 there were six steamers plying the Gareloch. The steamers were named after characters from novels by Sir Walter Scott, and a firm favourite was the *Lucy Ashton* (1888), which left Garelochhead Pier promptly at 7 a.m. and called at all eight piers on the route before starting the return voyage at noon. By the end of the 1930s the pier at Helensburgh had deteriorated to such an extent that only local steamers called. Silting up brought closure in 1952, but, lately, the pier repaired and the area dredged, the paddle-steamer *Waverley* (1946) has included Helensburgh on her summer runs, proving that a trip *doon the watter* has never really lost its appeal.

In a town whose charm is enhanced by its relationship with the Firth, it is regrettable that the shops on the all-important foreshore sadly fail to make real impact, lacking the uniformity of a waterfront, lined on the one side by modest, two-storey-and-attic properties, and on the other by a jolly esplanade. The ubiquitous awnings of a summer's day, the flagpoles and bandstands, the boat-hirers trading from the pier are gone. Extensive land reclamation has washed up a sea of tarmac – a sprawling car park at the corner of which architectural mediocrity looms large in the form of the Granary Restaurant, 1986.

Imperial Hotel, 12 West Clyde Street, *c.*1830 (*left*) Trim, black-and-white, with pronounced quoins and string-coursing, commendably restrained at street level. At **18** (victim of a malevolent dormer) stands a good red sandstone tenement built in 1909 by T & J Low of Greenock. At **20-23** is the 1933 art deco infill of **Woolworths**, battleship-grey and rather intimidated by the bulk of the corner building for the former **National Bank of Scotland**, 1928, A N Paterson & Stoddart. Now the offices of the **Helensburgh Property Centre**, the block has two virtually symmetrical street façades, each balanced around a chimneyed, gabled centrepiece – that on Clyde Street flanked by ornamental urns.

(1) *Quay c.1830.* (2) *Outdoor Swimming Pool.* (3) *Esplanade.* (4) *West Esplanade.* (5) *Waterfront c.1870.* (6) *Helensburgh by E A Walton, 1886*

Above *36 West Clyde Street.*
Right *74-78 West Princes Street*

Robert Wemyss appears to have settled in Helensburgh in 1896, having worked in Glasgow in the office of Burnet, Son & Campbell, where it is possible he may have met A N Paterson. Much in demand as an architect of distinctive, one-off villas, the style in which Wemyss chose to work fell somewhere between that of William Leiper and of Paterson and it is often difficult to distinguish among the three. Wemyss died in 1955.

62-66 West Princes Street

Helensburgh Pier
The first *ruckle of stanes*, a dyke constructed in 1810, never took the shape of the three breakwater walls to which the town plan of 1838 made optimistic allusion. Rebuilt 1859, enlarged 1871, the pier was superseded by the jetty at nearby Craigendoran, completed in 1882.

Esplanade, 1880s
Built by public subscription, the foreshore is grassed, floral and meticulously tended. At **No 36 West Clyde Street**, the former Bank of Scotland, 1876, by William Petrie, is jolly Scots Baronial with crow-steps and corbels. At the foot of **James Street** a red granite obelisk, monument to the aspirations and achievements of the marine engineer, **Henry Bell**, stands sentinel over the Firth.

Nos 74-78 West Princes Street, 1896, Robert Wemyss
A grey-harled tenement with stone dressings, brick panels and squat turreted corner. **62-66**, formerly Waverley Place, asymmetrical red sandstone façade with arched upper-floor windows and corbelled chimneypiece. Alongside, a convincing three-storey corner block combining well with the **West Kirk**, 1853, J W & J Hay, sensitively restored by the ubiquitous Wemyss after a fire in 1924. The church has that certain Presbyterian squatness, exaggerated by a buttressed broach spire on the south front (the firm's trademark). Exceptionally fine stained glass, including a memorial to Andrew Bonar Law, and a delicate, much-crocketed porch added in 1892 by William Leiper.

Colquhoun Square
Created from a quarry of red sandstone, recently given some sense of enclosure by Alan Berry's two 1980s brick housing developments. A flamboyant **post office**, 1893, designed by

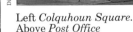

Left *Colquhoun Square.*
Above *Post Office*

W W Robertson, at **18 Colquhoun Street** is late Victorian with an elongated cupola. The **Bank of Scotland**, 1861, is enhanced by a good extension, 1982, within which a pyramid-type roof is supported off an ambitious umbrella structure designed by David Morgan.

At **8-12 West Princes Street**, 1911, W Hunter McNab, stand two bays of Jacobean-like exuberance – grey sandstone, gigantic chimney stacks, an exaggerated skyline and a crowd of clamouring, knobbly finials; the projecting ashlar teeth of an unfinished gable are sad reminders that the building was intended to sweep around the corner in a grand bellcapped tower. The tenement enjoys an easy friendship with William Tait's more controlled composition at **14-28**, dating from 1878.

Left & below *8-12 West Princes Street*

EAST BAY

This part of Helensburgh, where the early wealthy residents settled, now lacks the impact of its western counterpart, in part due to the breakdown of the grid-iron, but more to the industrial bias, given the area. Not only does the railway divide upper and lower Helensburgh east, but here, too, were once located the slaughterhouse, the gasworks, the steamie, an aerated mineral waterworks and a

Mitchell Library

Henry Bell (1767-1830) trained first in Glasgow, and then London, as a mill-wright, ship model-maker and engineer. He settled in Helensburgh during the late 1790s, disappointed by the Admiralty's refusal to investigate his proposals for steam navigation (this despite recommendations in his favour from Lord Nelson). In 1807, he became the town's first Provost and immediately sought to capitalise on Helensburgh's growing reputation for sea-bathing by building the paddle-steamer *Comet* in 1812 to link Glasgow, Greenock and Helensburgh. To his energies the town owes its early expansion. Bell worked on the supply of drinking water to Helensburgh from Glen Fruin. He was buried in the Parish Churchyard at Rhu, where the monument raised in his memory by Robert Napier takes pride of place.

East Bay

F distillery at the foot of Maitland Street. The gasworks remain, dominating the view from Craigendoran. **Clyde Street School** (*above*) 1903, A N Paterson, is slightly overwrought, its symmetrical street façade concentrated around a top-lit, gabled attic with Venetian window; on either side lead-topped ogee roofs prickling with starfish finials and spreading to pronounced bellcasts. The composition flows out to low, bellcapped octagonal classrooms. Two supporting lodges continue the theme.

East Princes Street bears the scars of Helensburgh's industrial heritage, although there is a notable block of 1931 burgh-built housing on the corner of Princes Street and **Adelaide Street**.

Queen's Court (formerly Queen's Hotel), East Clyde Street, 1808, Henry Bell; 1984, Baxter Clark & Paul
The brash brick of **Queen's Court** (flats) effects an overpowering addition to what remains of the former hotel. At the time of its conversion, its saving grace was a lively glass-

Drummond

and-timber entrance porch; the castellations had long been erased, the form of the original structure indistinct. The porch demolished, the once dazzlingly white stucco walls were painted, layers of history sealed beneath layers of unflattering terracotta.

Cromalt, 148 East Clyde Street, 1700; altered 1802, David Hamilton

Originally a farmhouse and home of novelist Neil Munro, the gracious Regency two-storey, elegant white stucco building sits back on a raised grassy platform above the water. The main body stretches into single-storey wings with pedimented pavilions and bowed ends. East is a gabled stables block with dainty, domed cupola and weather-vane.

Left *Cromalt*.
Above *Queen's Hotel*

Neil Munro (1864-1930), Inveraray lawyer's clerk turned romantic novelist and journalist, was in semi-retirement when he moved to Helensburgh. In his descriptive book *The Clyde* the author of the *Para Handy* tales described the town thus: *There is a certain air – not, strictly speaking, hauteur, let us call it dignity or self-respect – about Helensburgh which makes it stand aloof from the vulgar competition of other coast towns for popular recognition ... And although the burgh is, in a generous sense, a suburb of Glasgow, it is in secret communicable relation with the wilds.*

G **Rockland**, 150 East Clyde Street, 1854, Alexander Thomson

The house embraces the Greek detailing with which Thomson is often identified with a shallow pitched roof with understated bargeboards and oversized acroteria. Rough ashlar walling gives way to a window wall at upper level, the glazing with token

East Bay, mid 19th century

Rockland

subdivisions in the shape of dressed stone pilasters. In a town where compact Victorian villas were often later elongated to segregate ancillary accommodation, Rockland was conceived in that form, with the kitchen and servants' quarters contained in a long, low wing to the east. The finely chiselled porch is probably a later addition.

Tigh-na-Mara, 152 East Clyde Street, alterations 1905, William Leiper
Home to the playwright James Bridie (O H Mavor) during his last years, the house owes its present appearance of protruding bays, sandstone dressings, gargoyle-inhabited porch and voluminous red, rosemary-tiled roof to alterations by William Leiper. Somewhere within this harled villa hides an older house.

Below *Tigh-na-Mara.*
Bottom *Rockfort*

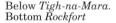

Rockfort, East Clyde Street, 1849
A jagged gabled composition heavy with Gothic overtones. The house, complete with brooding hoodmoulds and intricate bargeboards, features in many period illustrations of the east esplanade.

KIRKMICHAEL
Idealistic garden city development, much neglected. Begun by the Burgh Surveyor in 1935 with three blocks on **Kirkmichael Road**, featuring dormers, gablets, curious concrete balconies with sinuous ironwork, and glass blocks to stairhead windows. Work ceased on the outbreak of the Second World War. Afterwards, Stewart & Paterson developed **Ben Bouie Drive** and **Buchanan Road**, a series of tenements and cottages in revived

Scottish vernacular. At Ben Bouie Drive and **Stuckleckie Road** steep red-tiled mansards and peeping dormers mark the housing, while on Buchanan Road abrupt gablets and grey slate give the same plan-form a new guise. Harling enlivened by fanciful brick dressings, a turret on **Old Luss Road**, and on Kirkmichael Road, pediments and portholes.

Victoria Infirmary, 93 East King Street, 1895, William Leiper
A pleasing cottage hospital sited somewhat unreassuringly by the town cemetery. Trimmed in deep red sandstone, the building is scattered across the site but presents a composed entrance elevation with bellcapped bays, long ward wings and an asymmetrically set doorway. Interesting brick detailing in the **Nurses' Quarters**, 1939, Balfour & Stewart.

Top *Kirkmichael Road.* Above & left *Victoria Infirmary*

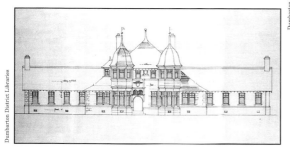

EASTEND PARK
A triangular expanse of parkland gifted to the town, above which **George Street** and **East Montrose Street** collide in an attempt to maintain the grid-iron layout despite the contrariness of the contours. The surrounding housing is notable for numerous post-Victorian extensions and alterations. Local architects Leiper, Wemyss and Paterson were responsible and, given the striking similarities in their work, the area has a homogeneity it might not otherwise have expected. Leiper's 1893 addition to **Rossland**, 19 East Montrose Street – slim, two-storey and vaguely oriental – ranks amongst the best.

The aptly named **Redcote, 23 Henry Bell Street**, 1881, T L Watson, is a tentative precursor of the half-timbered style practised with such relish by Leiper. **Bowhouse** on **Charlotte Street**, 1988, Tony Vogt, is outstanding – its great, timber-clad prow nosing its way out towards the view.

Bowhouse

The rambling Scots Gothic **Towerville**, 1858, John Honeyman, on the curve of **George Street**, is a combination of palatial sprawl and never-ending array of castellations, quatrefoils, hoodmoulds and buttressed bay windows. Immeasurably more romantic is the **lodge** peeping above the undergrowth.

Park Church, Charlotte Street, 1862, John Honeyman
An elegant Gothic composition culminating in a pencil-slim spire with open belfry. The interior, remodelled 1888, William Leiper, is divided into three aisles by stone arcades carried on columns of polished Peterhead granite. The rose window seems overwrought compared with the effortless Free Style tracery of the **RC Church of St Joseph**, 1911, C J Menart, on **Lomond Street**. No spire or tower, but a simple cruciform plan with side aisles and gabled stair towers flanking the twin entrances.

On **East King Street**, an intriguing, yet sadly neglected, 1936 council-built scheme in the familiar idiom of Stewart & Paterson; **Alma Place** is dully rendered, but the 35 houses, contained within three blocks linked by bogus arches, have a potential which a coat of white paint would do much to highlight. The courtyard elevations have stylised staircase bays with attractive lunette windows.

Top *Towerville*. Middle *Park Church*. Above *R C Church of St Joseph*. Right *Alma Place*

Registry Office

The self-effacing **Baptist Church**, 1886, D Abercrombie, has a chubby economical spire; the **Church of St Columba**, 1865, William Spence, is more assertive, its unusual Gothic tower terminating in a classical, balustraded upper stage. Charming **Registry Office**, 1890, Robert Wemyss, on **West King Street**.

Victoria Halls

Sinclair

Victoria Halls, Sinclair Street, 1887,
J & R S Ingram
Helensburgh's Town Hall, cut from hammer-
dressed ashlar is relieved by a series of perky
tourelles and a mansard-style tower, but
Victoria, frowning out from the hefty first-floor
balcony remains unamused. Adjacent, on the
edge of **Milligs Burn**, are the remains of **Malig
Mill**, where a grindstone and three engraved
roundels commemorate the twice rebuilding of
this once vital meal mill and meeting place.

Hermitage Park
Public park, created by the Town Council from
the grounds of the now demolished Hermitage
House. The flywheel from **Comet**'s first engine,
and the anvil on which parts of the engine were
forged can be found within. An exquisite walled
garden contains A N Paterson's domed and
gilded **War Memorial** of 1923. Diminutive
sheltered housing, 1991, McGurn, Logan,
Duncan & Opfer on Sinclair Street.

McGurn Logan Duncan & Opfer

Left *War Memorial.* Above
*Sheltered Housing, Sinclair
Street*

Dumbarton District Libraries

Above *Moorgate*.
Right *Extension to Arden*

Alexander Nisbet Paterson
(1862-1947) provided one of the
links between Helensburgh and
the Glasgow Boys. His brother
James was a painter and his
wife Maggie the young sister of
the artist J Whitelaw Hamilton.
Amongst their friends they
could count James Guthrie,
E A Walton and Joseph
Crawhall. Paterson was a
watercolourist, an excellent
draughtsman, and an architect
whose best work was in a cosy
Scots Renaissance style. He
trained at the Ecole des Beaux-
Arts in Paris in 1886, joining
Burnet, Son & Campbell on his
return and setting up on his
own account in 1892. In 1897
he moved to Helensburgh,
building first the Turret at 22
Millig Street, and then, four
years later, the Longcroft,
where he remained until his
death. He was seldom without
work, taking Campbell Douglas
into partnership in 1903, and D
M Stoddart in 1919. Paterson
was responsible for a number of
public buildings in the town,
but it is his domestic work
which makes the greater
contribution to the
architectural heritage of
Helensburgh.

Right *43 Alma Crescent*.
Below *Greenpark*

K **Moorgate**, 4 Albert Street, 1903, A N Paterson
Large, harled villa in Scots vernacular with
scrolled skew-puts, crow-steps and flush
dormers. Shaped gable on the entrance
elevation and a curious Venetian window.

Arden, Alma Crescent, notable for its flat-
roofed extension, 1916, by Stewart & Paterson
with precise ashlar walling and Lutyens-
inspired stone-mullioned and leaded windows
in a flat, central bay.

L **English Villas**: 41, 43, 45 Alma Crescent,
1906-9, William Leiper
Charming composition of three houses for John
Jack, a local builder: **41** with red sandstone
base and chimneys, stone-mullioned and
transomed bays, and half-timbering, **43** with
chunky bargeboards and harled chimney
stacks; **45**, built last, a less expensive rendition
of 41, with a billiard room added by Leiper's
pupil (latterly partner), W Hunter McNab, in
1913.

M Uphill, a streamlined surprise at **Greenpark**,
11 East Abercromby Street, 1935, John S Boyd,
which was built on the foundations of Balvaird
destroyed by fire in 1932. A sleek newcomer in

primrose and lilac, the villa presents two faces: the powerful horizontality of the entrance façade swept round to the east gable in a deep, curving balcony and terrace, and, at the rear, tall, narrow windows in a soaring staircase tower.

In the grounds is Robert Sills's inspired office refurbishment of the former **stables** to Balvaird, 1910, lush yellow sandstone and a portly cupola by A N Paterson (*below*).

WEST END
The contour-responsive informality of the East End owed much to the revisions to the feuing plan made by William Spence in 1857. Spence introduced the crescent and curve, but his ambitious whorling street plans proved little match for the rigid chequerboard rhythm of the West End. Here, while density decreases the more distant the Firth becomes, the mathematical precision of the street pattern is reinforced by the regimental marching of flowering cherry, birch, rowan, hawthorn and lilac.

The land closest to the Clyde remains densely developed with only public buildings afforded open ground. Modern infill schemes such as the sheltered housing at **Waverley Court**, 1982, Baxter Clark & Paul, on **West King Street**, respect this trend with a strong street frontage enlivened by indents and outshots.

At the junction of **John Street** and **King Street**, the Gothic spire of the former **St Bride's Parish Church**, 1877, by John McLeod, (hall by Leiper, chancel by A N Paterson) exerts a calming influence on the fidgeting tenement alongside; replaces an iron church by Francis Morton of Liverpool. **27 John Street**, 1896, Robert Wemyss, lovely patchwork-quilt tenement with sandstone bays, grey harling and an arched ground floor sheltering under a cornice on corbels.

John Logie Baird
(1888-1945)
Born at The Lodge, 27 West Argyle Street, Baird had demonstrated by 1900 his flair for electrical engineering by installing the first electric lighting in Helensburgh, in his own home. Moving to London, he first televised a human face on 2 Oct. 1925, making a public demonstration of this pioneering achievement in Jan. 1926. Baird made little out of his invention; he turned down a large sum of money for the patent and remained untempted by William Chrysler, the American magnate. Then, in 1937, he faced the disappointment of having his system turned down by the Television Advisory Committee for use by the BBC, the EMI-Marconi system being chosen instead. A secretive man, Baird continued to experiment with video recordings, three-dimensional colour television, and radar. He was buried in Helensburgh, where he is commemorated by a bust in Hermitage Park, and a stained-glass window in the West Kirk.

Below *Waverley Court.* Bottom *St Bride's Parish Church*

Above *Gargoyle, William Street.*
Below *72-76 King Street.*
Middle *Corner of Montrose
Street / Glasgow Street.* Bottom
40A Glasgow Street. Right *Glen
Kin*

N **St Michael's & All Angels**, William Street, 1882, Sir Robert Rowand Anderson (*left*) Spreading, solid French Gothic, the buttressed swagger enhancing the crossing of Princes Street and William Street; the tower added in 1930. The finest feature of the church is the intricately carved tympanum from which exquisite effigies of man and beast loftily ignore the two sneering, spitting gargoyles who threaten their peace from the dormers of the villa diagonally opposite. The discreet little **First Church of the Christ Scientist**, 1956, Margaret Brodie, sits nearby.

Rosebank, at **152** Princes Street secured its expansive grounds *c.*1830 before the street layout was established. To the rear a large extension, 1891, by William Leiper, pivots under a hefty, domed bay clad in red tiles and slumped low on timber brackets. At **121**, an early shore farm surviving as **Brandongrove** confirms the whitewashed appeal of the town's origins.

There is much to please the eye: the lookalike additions to **Rosemount**, 10 Argyle Street, on the right a canted bay in red tile and timber, 1895, by Leiper; on the left a flat bay on corbels, 1907, by Wemyss; Duncan McNaughton's 1901 Free Style consulting rooms and circular bay to **Rothiemay**, 30 Colquhoun Street, and decorative staircase, bays and ironwork to **Ericstane**, 7 Montrose Street, 1901; Leiper's banded stone additions of 1889 to **Glen Kin**, 76 John Street, a rotund chinaman-hatted tower in ochre and umber, and elaborate timber bays; a delightful terrace

at **72-76 King Street**, abundant with decorative ironwork; John McIntyre's tidy modern house at **40A Glasgow Street**; and Robert Wemyss's handsome villa of 1898 at the corner of Montrose Street and Glasgow Street, jigsaw-patterned red sandstone with harled upper storey and a stepping, stone-traceried staircase window.

UPPER WEST END

By 1865 the town boundaries had reached
Sutherland Street, and almost as far as
Millig Street. The twin, semicircular paths of
Upper and **Lower Sutherland Crescent**
(first envisaged by William Spence eight years
previously) were yet to be built; at odds with
the grid but no less formal. *En route* to the
ancient seat of Ardencaple, the grid gives its
last gasp.

William Leiper (1839-1916)
moved to Helensburgh from
Glasgow in the early 1870s and
became the town's most prolific
and influential architect. For a
brief period after his move he
abandoned architecture in
favour of painting. Leiper had
long been interested in applied
decoration; he was an admirer
of William Burges and a friend
of the decorative artist Daniel
Cottier, with whom he
collaborated on a number of
Anglo-Japanese projects which
included the interior of
Cairndhu (1871). After the
1880s his work was for the most
part in the domestic idiom,
latterly much inspired by
Richard Norman Shaw. Leiper
spent his last years tending his
roses at Terpersie (1871) and
was buried in the family grave
in Glasgow.

Mitchell Library

O **Terpersie**, 2 Upper Sutherland Street, 1871,
William Leiper
A reticent red and grey cottage which shares
the *shy and retiring disposition* of its architect
and original inhabitant. Fastidious detail in
and around the arched entranceway. The boar's
head whose snout protrudes above the hall
window may be descended from an ancestor
carved on Terpersie Castle, Aberdeenshire,
allegedly the home of Leiper's forefathers.
Leiper shrewdly feued the adjacent plot and
built **Rhu-Arden**, *c*.1873, a faithful
interpretation of Greek forms but for the
Roman porch. North on **Millig Street**, the
same architect's **Westermillig** (built as
Redholm) dates from the same period but
represents an emphatic return to Victorian
Gothic, with scalloped barge-boards and a
south-facing bay drawn into three peaks.

Canary Islands, Rowallan Street /
Millig Street, 1895, A N Paterson
Four model villas, one designed by the
architect for himself, their name derived from
the brilliant yellow of the original render; the

Left *Terpersie*. Below *Rhu-Arden*. Bottom *Canary Islands*

Dick

Dick

harling now pristine white. All four have split
pediments, red sandstone dressings and crow-
steps, and low dormers, all assembled
differently. Fifteen years later, Robert Wemyss
produced four villas of yellow stone bays, sandy
roughcast gablets and grey slate slopes at
61-67 John Street.

Clarendon, 89 James Street, 1888/91,
principally William Leiper
Two flamboyant French additions render the
original house unrecognisable; crenellations,
crow-steps and a clutch of chattering gargoyles
scrambling up the east tower. Better tempered
is the architect's onion-domed museum
extension, 1902, to **Marden House** at
68 Colquhoun Street.

Right *Longcroft*. Below
A N Paterson in his studio

P **Longcroft**, West Rossdhu Drive, 1901,
A N Paterson
Paterson's own house was *an expression of all he
felt about domestic architecture*, and represents
the apogee of his career. Close to the West
Highland Railway, 1894, access is at the end of
an interminably long road. In Longcroft Paterson
gave life to a composition which, if self-indulgent,
displays the conviction of a man who knows his
architectural roots. Particularly fine west
frontage, where the turret and tower are held in
thrall to an authoritatively shaped gable. Inside,
fireplaces by George Walton, plaster ceilings by
Bankart and painted glass. Snug children's
entrance on the south and, on either side of the
main entrance, their heads appear in carved
form.

UPPER TOWN

There is real architectural wealth on the hills of the Upper Town, although avaricious development on the east has tempered the effect, and expansion on the west is similarly detrimental. The Glade Estate has all but absorbed the six **Easterhill Road** villas, 1907-12, Mitchell & Whitelaw; Scots Renaissance designed to attract wealthy buyers to the ground adjacent to the Golf Course. On either side of Sinclair Street are quiet avenues, saturated in seasonal colour, commanding unrivalled views of the Clyde and Renfrewshire hills.

Below *The Hill House with (beyond) Drumadoon.* Bottom *The Hill House*

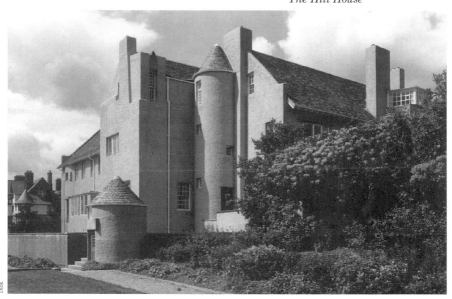

Q **The Hill House**, 8 Upper Colquhoun Street, 1902, Charles Rennie Mackintosh
On the edge of the Blackhill Plantation, The Hill House, built for publisher W W Blackie, is one of the great houses of 20th-century architecture. Plan-form much used on the lower slopes of the town, giving entry from the side, freeing the south-facing frontage to the benefit of the public rooms. Beyond this, references to Helensburgh's adopted vernacular are remote: blocky and Baronial, overtly Scottish in a neighbourhood where Tudor half-timbering is plentiful, clothed in sandy-grey harling with no colour or applied decoration for external effect. Particularly fine entrance façade, asymmetrical dual-chimneyed

The Hill House: Top *Drawing room*. Above *Shower*. Right *Detail, window catch*

gable framed by the whorl of the gates at the end of the drive. If the exterior seems severe despite the skillful massing, the magnificently crafted interior is in delightful contrast. There is interplay of light and dark in the stained timber of the hall, relieved by tiny inserts of coloured glass and stencilwork and next in the deep hue of the drawing room ceiling which bears down on the delicate decoration of the white walls and fireplace. Upstairs, lightness predominates in the elegance of the master bedroom, pink, white and pewter, the original stencilwork restored. The attention to detail throughout is all-encompassing, the integration of architecture, decoration, furniture and fittings masterly. Saved for posterity by the Royal Incorporation of Architects in Scotland in 1972.
Now owned by the National Trust for Scotland and open to the public

Drumadoon, 17 Upper Colquhoun Street, 1903, William Leiper
A restless mass where skill in the composition is revealed best around the ogee-arched entrance at the rear beside which protrudes a turret sheltering a curious, hanging bell. Downhill, **Lynton**, formerly Polkemmet, 1908, Leiper, simpler, less frenetic and implicitly allied to his English villas in the east end of town.

Dhuhill Drive
Three elongated villas catch the eye: **Brincliffe**, 1907, by Frank Burnet, Boston & Carruthers; **Graycourt** (formerly **Courtallam**), 1910, A N Paterson, somewhat experimental, with a curious, gabled entrance tower; and the heavily timbered **Lethamhill**, 1914, by John Burnet & Son. **Braeriach**, 4 Upper Colquhoun Street, 1908, a mature composition by Robert Wemyss. The capacious
R **Red Towers**, 1898, Leiper, is an ornamental mansion house with salty-red sandstone towers, bays and balconies formed beneath a drape of green slate, out of which peep half-timbered dormers.

S **The White House**, 15 Upper Colquhoun Street, 1899, M H Baillie Scott
Chaste cubic composition commissioned by H S Paul harmonising with its neighbours through the use of whitewash and red tile. Free-form layout (championed in Helensburgh by Leiper), entered from the rear, with seaward spaces enlivened by intimate little ingle-nooks. The double-height entrance hall is gone, and the attendant vertical stretch of glazing (which gave prescient simplicity to the south front) subdivided. The external finish remains

Top *Drumadoon*. Middle *Graycourt*. Above *Red Towers*. Left *The White House*

The White House by Baillie Scott and **The Hill House** by Mackintosh make for interesting comparison; together they brought the first signs of modernism to the slopes of upper Helensburgh. Their work has been assessed alongside before – in 1901 the *Zeitschrift für Innen-Dekoration* sponsored an international competition for the design of a *Haus eines Kunstfreundes* – an art lover's house. Both architects entered, and while no first prize was awarded, Baillie Scott won second place. Mackintosh had been unable to complete his entry and was requested to submit further drawings. On so doing he was awarded a special prize, and a building based on the design has now been erected (despite reservations from purists) in Glasgow's Bellahouston Park.

striking: no barge-boards, copes or skews, no sills or hoodmoulds – only token overhanging eaves betraying English origins. Decorative hopperheads, coloured leaded glass and tiny peep windows on the east gable snuggle up on either side of the chimney breast.

Downhill, **Whincroft**, 2 Upper Colquhoun Street, 1914, A N Paterson, is less whimsical than his earlier commissions. **Lennox Drive West**, further south, has more white harl and red roofs; **Clairinch**, 1904, H & D Barclay, is the most voluminous. Best of all is the elegant 1930s symmetry of **No 14**, **Broom Cottage**, 1934, by A Gardner, Gardner & McLean.

Munro Drive West is enhanced by two exceptionally picturesque Arts & Crafts compositions.

T **Brantwoode**, 4 Munro Drive West, 1895, William Leiper
A romantic vision of banded chimneystacks, stone relieving arches and buttresses, a Romeo & Juliet balcony clad in red fishscale tiles, mock half-timbered gablets, stone-transomed bays, and intricate leaded glass. Private, yet welcoming; inside, library, lounge and dining-room interconnect (as do the bedrooms above) and have outstanding feature fire surrounds – one with the original blue and gold embossed wall covering by William Morris. The hall fireplace carving sums up the sentiment: *In the world a home, in the home my world.*

Brantwoode

Strathmoyne, 6 Munro Drive West, 1899,
Robert Wemyss
With a powerful, protruding entrance tower
within which rises a grand staircase,
Strathmoyne repeats details Wemyss had
sought to perfect the previous year at Redcliffe
(now **Rokneys**), a trim villa at the junction of
Munro Drive East and **Sinclair Street**, with
an impressive repertoire of fanciful windows
and brilliant red vertical tiling wrapping
around the upper storey.

Sinclair Street
The former Luss Road abandons the
north/south axis at **Tordarroch**, 1883, a
characteristically ornamental array of
timbering and tile by Leiper, curving east, past
Dhuhill Lodge, 1898, also by Leiper, and
Dhuhill (John Dingwall?), its chilly composure
at odds with the cheeky charm of the lodge. A
tiny, heavily wooded public park, the **Walkers'
Rest**, hides the rumbustious **Albion Lodge**,
1883; more Leiper, with a billiard room and
garage extension, 1910, by Stewart & Paterson.

Mains Hill Reservoir, established 1866,
augmented by a filter works and settlement
tanks in 1925. Remains can still be seen
opposite the well-ordered **Ardluss**, 1900, one of
Leiper's last, most refined compositions. On the
northern outskirts, past **Millig Toll**, is the
house in the wood, **Drum-Millig**, 1909,
A N Paterson; a curious, harled villa with a
walnut-timbered interior and exaggerated
coved lounge ceiling recalling the splendours
of Longcroft (see p.82).

RHU ROAD LOWER
In the 1930s the land between Helensburgh
West and Rhu was developed as small feus
derived from the grounds of **Ardencaple
Castle**. A bulky retaining wall with a 1578
cartouche, and the north-west Argyll tower
survived demolition, the square, battlemented
tower used as a mount for transit lights to
assist sailors to navigate Rhu Narrows.

Top *Strathmoyne.* Middle above
Rokneys. Middle below *Albion
Lodge.* Above *Drum-Millig*

In 1919, the Town Council selected the site
south of the castle wood (of which there is but
sparse reminder) for their first municipal
housing development, **Ardencaple Quadrant**.
Designed by Stewart & Paterson with
characteristic detailing of gablets, dormers and
harling, it provided homes for men returning
from the First World War.

Ardencaple Castle c.1930

The Clan MacAuley, whose family seat was at Ardencaple Castle, settled as landowners in the area around the 13th century.

Auley, last of the lairds of MacAuley, abandoned the castle as a roofless ruin, whereupon it was purchased by Archibald, 3rd Duke of Argyll around 1752, passing to John, 4th Duke, in 1761. While parts of the castle may date to 1249, to *the ancient Fort of Arncaple with its dungeons, and tunnel under the sea to Rosneath*, the building demolished in 1957 for a naval housing estate had been substantially altered, principally by Robert Adam, who had prepared plans for alterations to the original *tower fortalice manor place of Ardincaple* in 1764, when the castle was an arcaded U-plan château. Further proposals in 1772 comprised a west wing made up of circular banded towers (latterly with corbelled parapets) whose importance – representing as they did the evolvement of Adam's *castle-style* design – is only now being acknowledged, long after their disappearance.

V **Kidston Estate**, 1930s
In 1936, the expansive castle lawn was subdivided into tiny plots. In the sullen shadow of the massive retaining wall (said to represent the original coastline) were built a host of bungalows and villas for builders Charles Murrie of Kirkintilloch, and Thomas Watson of Largs and Helensburgh. **3 Kidston Drive**, 1939, is an archetypal 1930s house: white, curved corners and windows, a flat roof and streamlined horizontality. Behind, **18 Loch Drive**, 1938, has retained its elegantly proportioned metal windows which lend subtle transparency to the corners of a white cube.

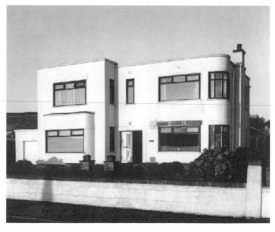

3 Kidston Drive

W **Cairndhu**, Rhu Road Lower, 1871,
William Leiper
Built for John Ure of Glasgow, a grain miller and
merchant, who became Lord Provost of the city,
and whose son became Lord Strathclyde. Grand
château in the manner of François I, with
outstanding interior, resulting from collaboration
between Leiper and the stained-glass artist,
Daniel Cottier. Despite conversion to a nursing
home, there remains much timber panelling, a
series of exceptional stained-glass windows
depicting truth, beauty, love, audacity *et al.*, and
in the original drawing room ceiling – *the finest
individual item of Anglo-Japanese in Scotland* –
gold on black, sunflowers and songbirds.

X **Dalmore**, Rhu Road Lower, 1873,
William Leiper
Crowsteps and crowned and carved dormers
combine to articulate the seaward façade, the
bare scattering of windows giving a grand,
impregnable effect. The flushed pink stonework
summons up a haughty demeanour. Less
severe are two **lodges** marking the waterfront
boundary of the estate.

Top *Cairndhu*. Middle *Original
drawing room ceiling, Cairndhu.*
Above *Dalmore*

Y **Ardencaple Hotel**, early 19th century
A striking three-storey block with balustraded
parapet and ornamental urns, flanked on
either side by protruding, pedimented pavilions
with arched panels and orderly black
trimmings. Used as a posting inn on the road
between Glasgow and Inveraray, it tells less
about the model town on whose shores it sits
than about the architecture of the older town
for which passing coaches were bound. An eye-
catching boundary marker at the meeting of
Helensburgh and the village of Rhu.

Ardencaple Hotel

Dumbarton District Libraries

Top *Rhu Bay.* Above *Rhu Parish Church*

Dick

RHU (ROW)

The original parish of Row was one of twelve in Dunbarton. The land, for the most part, was owned by the ancient family of Lennox, whose seat was at Faslane. In 1648, the parish was given independence when MacAulay of Ardencaple offered to finance the construction of a small church and manse. The site lay along the curve of the bay south of the shingle stretch at the mouth of the Gareloch; hence, Rhu – from the Gaelic *rudha*, meaning a promontory. In time, the nucleus of cottages, parish kirk, ferry and school developed into a more extensive village of considerable charm.

Rhu Parish Church, 1851, William Spence
A striking Gothic silhouette soars above an attractively jumbled churchyard. Honeyman & Keppie, who lengthened the nave in 1891, left William Spence's pinnacled octagonal tower untouched; a telescopic affair rising through a square, buttressed lower stage to culminate in an elegant pierced coronet. A romantic, ivy-clad fragment of the second kirk survives close to the entrance at the base of the tower.

Rhu Village

The first thatched shore cottages have disappeared, but **Rhu Inn** remains, and the housing on the lip of the bay still has an appealing ruralism. Above the **School Road** villas is the whitewashed **Cumberland Terrace**, *c.*1870, the persistent rhythm of elongated timber porches and dormers barely restrained by two stocky end pavilions. On

Cumberland Terrace

Dick

Hall Road, the hesitant Arts & Crafts of the local **Community Education Centre**, 1905, deserves a second look, while **19-35 Braehouse**, 1939 – Burgh-built baby-Baronial by Joseph Weekes – scrambles up the hill from the shore road in a cosy composition of gables, towers and piended dormers.

Rhu Point

The unpredictable South Narrows between the twin promontories of Rhu and Rosneath create the illusion that the banks are within striking distance of each other. In the heyday of the Dumbarton horse and cattle fairs, animals brought from Argyllshire to Rosneath would circumvent the 10-mile trip around the head of the loch by crossing this short stretch of water. Row Point served as pasture, the land dubbed Ferry Acres.

The *bleak and unpromising aspect* of this grazing ground lay unrealised until 1849, when the Italianate mansion **Rosslea** was completed and a plantation of fir trees installed. The tower and rhythmically arched garden frontage remain as part of a hotel. Similarly, the neighbouring **Ardenvohr**, 1858, has lost its voluminous hothouses and slated tower, but retains a degree of Scots Baronial *hauteur* as the headquarters of the Royal Northern & Clyde Yacht Club. A little to the north, crow-steps, ball-finials and strapwork reappear on a courtyard building which, in turn, is linked to an unusual octagonal bastion on the loch shore.

Ardenconnel House, *c.*1790,
possibly David Hamilton

Of the *marine mansions* whose quiet presence provide backdrop to the village, the earliest was **Ardenconnel**. Andrew Buchanan, a Glasgow merchant, bought the estate and the neighbouring **Lettrowalt** and **Blairvaddick** from the luckless MacAulays of Ardencaple. Buchanan built a handsome two-storey house on raised basement whose dressed stone margins and harled and limewashed façades provided a model for the mansions of Rhu. Originally a symmetrical frontage with projecting wings and Venetian windows, the entrance elevation still carries conviction in its Corinthian-columned porch. Some distance behind, coach buildings embrace a sequestered courtyard.

Top *19-35 Braehouse.* Middle above *Ardenvohr.* Middle below *Loch shore bastion behind Ardenvohr.* Above *Ardenconnel House*

G Langmuir

Top *Rhu Pier c.1906*. Above
Yachting on the Gareloch

Dumbarton District Libraries

*The summer of 1510 was
particularly hot, and a school of
basking sharks invaded the
Gareloch to feed on an
abundance of herring. Although
these sharks do not attack man,
they were a sufficient menace to
fishing boats, but worse was to
come with the arrival of a
Saurian monster with a long,
straight, giraffe-like neck,
having a tail like that of a
crocodile, that could break an
oak tree. Tradition recounts that
it travelled at great speed. It did
everything horrible except spit
fire from its ugly jaws. Everyone
was panic-stricken, and knelt on
the shores praying to be
delivered from this evil
leviathan of the depths of the
ocean.*
J Arnold Fleming, *Helensburgh
and the Three Lochs*, 1956

Bought by the Colquhouns of Luss and then, in
1899, established as the Scottish holiday guest-
house of the Co-operative Holidays Association,
the building survived a fire in 1907, later to be
subdivided into private flats.

Pier Road
The attractions of Rhu as a setting for palatial
country residences became more apparent on
completion of the quay in 1835. The pier, the
first on the Gareloch, was located at the foot of
the beech-lined avenue leading to Ardenconnel.
The pier is now part of **Rhu Marina**, and the
avenue survives as **Pier Road**.
An elevated terrace of ground at the foot of the
road provided the dramatic setting for
Rowmore, 1831, where the artist James
Guthrie retired in 1915 to paint *Some Statesmen
of the Great War*. A curious L-shaped Scots
Gothic composition, now with modern
conservatory, the house enjoys panoramic views
framed in the whorls of a cast-iron balustrade.
The cream harling, ashlar dressings, stone-
mullioned and transomed windows and
recurring gables and gablets typify this and
other successive villas in the area.

Dick

Rowmore

Glenarn Road

Leads first to **Glenarn**, outstanding for its collection of rare rhododendrons, and then to **Invergare**, the mock Scots Baronial mansion built in 1855 by architect James Smith for himself. Stridently vertical, with tall windows, squared bays, ornamental turrets and crow-stepped gablets, the house is cumbersome, but enlivened to the rear by a stocky entrance tower added in 1923.

Torwoodhill Road

The squared, side-lit bays which protrude from the south front of Invergare occur again on the principal façade of the nearby **dower-house**. **Carbeth**, also by Smith, is this time an elegant Italianate composition, small, but with good plasterwork and a spritely little cupola. Next door, **Torwood House** shares the same flat bay windows, but has hood moulds, a rustic entrance porch, and a large west wing with battlemented parapets.

South lies **Hazelwood House**, and its attendant outbuildings; good gateposts, half-timbered additions and an attractive, curving stables and cottage block at the road's edge. Downhill is **Cliffton**, an impeccably mannered Italianate villa with arched entrance loggia and an eaves gutter dotted with ornament. At the foot of the lawn, on an adjacent feu, stands **Auchenlea**, 1981, Ian Smith, a modern triangular villa with a generous, southerly aspect and a tile-hung, timber balcony.

Lagarie, 1901, A N Paterson

The tortuous descent of Torwoodhill Road passes the entrance to **Torwoodhill**, c.1840 – a Scots Gothic confection in black and white of

Top *Invergare*. Middle *Outbuildings, Hazelwood House*. Above *Auchenlea*. Left *Lagarie*

Top *Armadale Villa*. Middle *Tigh Gael*. Above *Aros*

Smugglers' Glen, now the site of a large naval housing estate, was once notorious for illicit whisky distillation. **Broomieknowe** and **Aldonaig**, on either side of the mouth of **Whistler's Burn**, formed the headquarters of a large company of distillers, and the necessary coals, barrels and stores of malt would be landed by boat in the small cove where the burn disgorged into the Gareloch. The many-gabled Aldonaig is the sole survivor of this period; Broomieknowe has gone, as have the original workmen's cottages and the stone-built smugglers' still.

Ardlarich

towers, tourelles and lozenge slatework – before reaching the site of **Lagarie**. Despite its overly derivative homage to R Norman Shaw, this former children's home – now private flats – has some good bulbous bays and a delightfully half-timbered attic storey.

While soft white harling and grey sandstone margins identify Lagarie as a youthful, distant cousin of the Rhu lineage, the parent tongue is spoken more eloquently at **Armadale Villa**, an exceptionally elegant gabled building erected on the field once known as Lagarie Croft. Longer, and with a lead-capped trellis veranda and gabled half-dormers is the nearby **Artarman**: an economic composition enlivened by purposeful Gothic finials.

Station Road
Two good modern houses and the notable corner bastion of **Dunard** (most likely A N Paterson) provide the highlights on the road to the hill farm of Torr. The blue brindle brick of **Orchard House**, 1973, C R Kelly, is well suited to the crisp, angular design and period detailing. At **Tigh Gael**, 1976, Fred Walker, a powerful, brooding statement: a great slate ski-slope of a roof projecting out over a first-floor balcony.

Aros Road
Ardconnel Lodge, a whitewashed pedimented cottage at the foot of Aros Road, is imbued with all the romanticism associated with those bygone days when *to be a smuggler was a man's job, and no disgrace*. **Aros**, 1883, William Leiper, is of a different period; medium-sized and whinstone-built with half-timbered, partly tiled gables and a good porch. Nearby is the immaculately thatched roof of **Ardlarich**, 1937, a cosy L-shaped house with peeping dormers, period chimney stacks and a pleasing lich-gate.

SHANDON

Originally one of the ancient strongholds of the Earls of Lennox (*Sean Dun* is Gaelic for old fort), modern Shandon threads its way along the shores of the Gareloch from the outskirts of Rhu to Faslane Bay; the A814, widened and rerouted in 1969, bustles through this rural fringe.

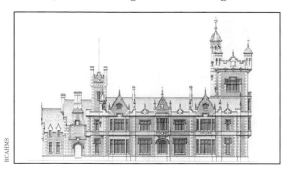

RCAHMS

West Shandon, 1852, J T Rochead (*above*)
Jagged, Scots-Jacobethan of palatial proportions commissioned by Robert Napier to house his collection of books, art works and exotic plants. In the art gallery were hung paintings by Rembrandt, Rubens and Raphael, and in the extensive garden ponds and greenhouses were cultivated rare species of plantlife fetched to Shandon by David Livingstone. After Napier's death in 1876, the mansion re-opened as the Shandon Hydropathic, complete with Russian, Turkish and saltwater swimming baths. Prosperity failed to return after the First World War, and the grounds were finally cleared in 1960 as part of the development of the Clyde Submarine Base. A beautiful **lodge** and the original **garden wall** with one extant bartizan remain on the old shore road.

Old Shandon Free Church, 1844
Relieved of its steeple and spirelet as part of a transformation into four luxury flats, the

Robert Napier, one of the leading marine engineers and shipbuilders of his era, was born in Dumbarton in 1791. By the age of 15 he was apprenticed to his blacksmith father, leaving for Edinburgh five years later to work for lighthouse engineer Robert Stevenson. After a period of employment with William Lang of Glasgow, Napier established his own business in Greyfriars' Wynd as an engineer and blacksmith. By 1824 he had moved to Camlachie Foundry, alongside his cousin David, and had manufactured the first marine engine, for the paddle-steamer *Leven*. The engine outlived three successive hulls and is today preserved in Dumbarton. By 1828 the firm had established the Vulcan Foundry, to which was added the engine works of Lancefield in 1835. Between 1840 and 1865, in addition to the manufacture of engines, Napier was building the famous iron ships of the Cunard fleet. *It was an absolute guarantee of the highest order that a ship had been constructed by Mr Napier's firm.*

Below *Lodge, Shandon Hydropathic.* Left *Shandon from the pier*

Dumbarton District Libraries

Dick

95

squatness of the building owes more to the fact that tower, transepts, stone porch and buttresses were not added until 1883. The conversion was not unkind, although the War Memorial was relocated somewhat rudely to make way for an elevated car park.

Kirk Brae clambers steeply uphill to **Braidhurst**, the modern corner pavilion of a low, whitewashed row of older cottages. Tucked beneath the eaves is a brightly coloured bird, the eagle who talks to the north-west wind to ensure that the roof will not blow off. Carved by Michael Henderson, who designed this imaginative cornerpiece in 1977, the bird scowls fiercely at those who attempt the climb.

Blairvadach, *c*.1850, J T Rochead
The sum of the parts is hardly subtle; a good entrance porch with battlemented parapet and elaborately crafted doorway leads into a three-storey Scots Baronial wing with crow-steps and turrets and, after dropping into a two-storey bay with thistle-topped dormers, ends in a huge square keep with heavy machicolations, a pronounced window bay with balcony, and a corner tower with ogee roof – and this only on the south front. Behind are stables and outhouses with more crow-steps and towers. Inside, the plasterwork and panelling perpetrate the same entertaining assault on the senses.

Top *(Former) Free Church.*
Above *Carved bird on Braidhurst*

Below & right *Blairvadach*

Built for Sir James Anderson, Glasgow's Lord Provost between 1848 and 1851, the house passed into the hands of the Donaldson shipping family. It is now run as a children's home.

Croy is close by, begun in 1834 by Sinclair of Caithness; a large, irregularly gabled house with ornamental bargeboards and stone margins. The Gothic entrance arch is repeated on the little **gate-lodge**. On the seaward side of the road is the **Gullybridge House Nursing Home**, a former fishing lodge smart in black-and-white. **Gareside Cottage**, the gamekeeper's house on the original Stuckie Estate, is more of an anomaly – an English Arts & Crafts cottage built in London brick with Cumberland green peggies covering the roof and corbie-stepped chimney stacks.

Top *Croy*. Above *Gullybridge House Nursing Home*. Left *Gareside Cottage*

The old shore road is in part retained, giving some respite from the seemingly relentless passage of traffic along the lochside. **Chapelburn**, peeping out above a privet barrier, is a small villa with a long trellis veranda and a trio of gabled attic dormers. **Letrault**, 1855, extended 1864, is bigger, with the bonus of an elegant conservatory and squat, stone-trimmed central tower.

Linnburn, 1836, 1884

A long, gabled house, harled and with Gothic features, it stands high above the road behind a sturdy stone balustraded parapet. Begun by Samuel McCall, a Glasgow merchant, *who was very particular in the straight line of his avenue, the formation of his walls, and the symmetry of his garden.* Uphill, **Linnburn Cottage**, the original stables block was creatively converted for T Campbell Lawson when he sold The Hill House in Helensburgh (see pp.83-4) in 1972.

Glenfeulan

A lovely colonial-style house in pale peach harling and yellow sandstone, single storey raised up on a semi-basement. The central portion has canted bays and a simple pierced parapet at roof level on which are perched fat

Below *Letrault*. Bottom *Linnburn*

figurative urns. The right-hand wing is linked to a protruding conservatory while the stables block behind combines terraces and tower to enclose a simple courtyard. **Cragmhor**, *c*.1830, on the adjoining feu, is a stylish Georgian villa with a (now detached) Gothic winter garden.

Shandon House, 1849, Charles Wilson
No amount of abuse during its former role as St Andrew's List D School can detract from the picturesque nature of the composition. Incorporating the remains of a plainer mansion, it is a romantic, idealised evocation of the revived Baronial style, all battlemented parapets, bartizans and belvederes, corbels, crow-steps, strapwork and water spouts, heraldic devices (the 1800 datestone is a misnomer), turrets, tourelles and finials. The illusion is heightened by a great cloak of ivy which blurs the details and suggests great age: ironically, time stands still for the house as it awaits a new use.

Above *Cragmhor*.
Right *Shandon House*

Faslane was absorbed by the Royal Engineers' **Military Port No 1** during the Second World War. Used principally for the shipment of men and materials as part of the North African and Normandy campaigns, the ground was transformed into a railway marshalling yard, six 500-ft-deep water berths, 27 cranes and a floating dry-dock. At around the same time the Royal Air Force established an experimental station for sea-planes at Rhu, and the American Navy requisitioned Rosneath as a naval base. After the war, Faslane was used as a shipbreakers' yard, this in turn closing as part of the expansion of the Royal Navy's **Clyde Submarine Base**.

FASLANE
Faslane was formerly a bay of considerable beauty, although once James IV had used the Gareloch as a base for his incipient navy, it was only a matter of time before the abnormal depth of the waters and the shelter afforded by the surrounding hills marked the spot for further naval development.

Of the 12th-century **Faslane Castle**, part of the earldom of Lennox, there remains a grassy motte close to the crossing of the West Highland Railway and **Faslane Burn**. The medieval remains of **Faslane Chapel**, two lancet windows in the gable of a single, roofless chamber dedicated to St Michael, survive in the village cemetery. Lord Darnley, whose family inherited the Lennox Estates, was christened here. Buried in the cemetery are the dead of the submarine *K13*, which sank in Faslane Bay on 29 Jan. 1917 during her trials.

Belmore, remodelled 1856
Meticulously restored for use as offices by the Property Services Agency in 1984; famed for its distinctive rock gardens which are, alas, now gone. A great mansion grown from a small house – now with Italianate tower and campanile, and decorative window hoods and consoles. It is barely visible at the heart of the expansive **Clyde Submarine Base**.

GLEN FRUIN

Evidence of depopulation is strong; a thriving crofting community has been reduced to a scattered series of stone-built farm buildings whose scrubby pastures have in time been consolidated into the Luss Estates. Two ancient chapels, the larger dedicated to St Bride, have disappeared, although a cross slab remains adjacent to the 1840 schoolhouse at **Black Bridge**, and there are the barest suggestions of a graveyard in a field next to **Ballyvoulin Farm**.

Strone House, closest to the exit of the glen above Faslane, is a U-shaped courtyard building, harled and half-timbered, matched by two handsome stone and slated barns. Close by, a little above the **Fruin Water**, is a simple raised stone commemorating the bloody battle of 1603 between MacGregors and Colquhouns.
Smuggling provided the locals with a lucrative substitute for crofting during the 18th and 19th centuries. The whitewashed cottage of **Crosskeys**, prominent still on the road from Luss to Helensburgh, was conveniently located to serve as a licensed house.

Top *Faslane Chapel*. Above *Sundial, Faslane Cemetery*

Glen Fruin

Bannachra Castle

Garelochhead's one claim to notoriety occurred on Sunday 22 Aug. 1853 when the Clyde steamship *Emperor* attempted to land its passengers at the pier. The local proprietor, Sir James Colquhoun, disapproved strongly of Sabbath sailings and had engineered to have the jetty barricaded with *boxes, barrels and gangways*. Despite this, the crew were able to make their way ashore by attacking the laird's supporters with a *fusillade of coals, bottles, potatoes and turnips*. Sir James later took his case to court and succeeded in having the rights of private owners of piers confirmed.

Bannachra Castle, *c.*1512
At the foot of **Ben Bowie**, a fortified house built by the Colquhouns, ruinous now but deduced by MacGibbon and Ross to have been three storeys high with crow-stepped gables, still with some good-sized windows complete with shot-holes under. Here was assassinated Sir Humphrey Colquhoun, shot with an arrow as he ascended to bed, his route illuminated by a treacherous servant to the MacGregors outside. Once in the hands of the rival clan the castle was unceremoniously destroyed.

GARELOCHHEAD

Garelochhead straddles the boundary between the ancient parishes of Row and Rosneath; a semicircular clutch of cottages and villas at whose pier no fewer than six different steamers called regularly during the summer seasons of the early 1850s. Development since this heyday of the *Gearr loch* has been minimal, and while housing has taken root on the slopes of **Feorlinbreck**, the pier has long since crumbled.

The **Parish Church**, 1838, has a vernacular austerity – harled walls, stone dressings, tall, pointed windows and a Gothic bellcote. Church and churchyard are diminished in impact by the savage swathe of the passing A814, as are the nearby single-storey cottages. One small dwelling, **Lilybank**, shows some spirit in the form of a strange, fortified entrance complete with heavily hinged door, slit quatrefoil window and tiny, wooden gargoyles, and William Leiper's bonny **Garelochhead Primary School**, 1895, survives as part of the **Outdoor Centre**.

Below *Parish Church*. Right *(Former) Primary School*

Garelochhead

On **Station Road**, the timeless quality of the village has been preserved. Here, within earshot of a trickling burn, a contemplative council-built development by Joseph Weekes at **Nos 1-8**, *c.*1940, with scalloped corner doorways and central gablets, co-exists harmoniously with century-old shops and housing.

Further uphill, past a much elevated terrace of railwaymen's brick cottages, stands the **Stationmaster's House**, 1894, Robert Wemyss, almost urbane in its timber and red sandstone trimmings. A precarious series of steps gives access to the station – an island-platform building with glazed end screens and an overhanging concave roof, clad in wooden shingles imported from Switzerland.

From this heady location a grand panoramic scene unfolds: in the distance, the hump of **Creachan Mor** seen in silhouette behind the Rosneath peninsula; closer, in the village below, a glimpse of the gleaming shark's fin rooflight of **Our Lady Star of the Sea RC Chapel**, 1964, Thomas Cordiner, at Feorlinbreck.

Round the head of the loch are more villas, none quite as openly appreciative of the potential of the location as **Taliesin West**. Self-built by architect Robert McLaren and completed in 1980, this cedar and concrete split-level house is worthy homage to Frank Lloyd Wright and commendably uncompromising given the prominence of the site.

A trio of Scots Gothic villas stand close to the water, at the foot of the **Dahlandhui Burn**: **Rockville**, now a home for the elderly, **Dahlandhui Hotel** and **Carloch** were built in the 1860s for the brothers McCall. There is a gazebo in the garden of the hotel and some

The West Highland Railway was opened in 1894 and runs from Craigendoran to Fort William. It was largely the work of the engineer Charles De Neuville Forman, a partner in Forman & McCall of Glasgow, who was recorded in his obituary in 1901 as having *introduced ... the island platform ... giving a wayside station an aesthetic picturesqueness foreign to the prevailing dinginess of most of our country railway buildings.* Garelochhead and Arrochar & Tarbet are two of the few remaining examples of the *Swiss-style* architecture adopted on this spectacular and scenic route. The stations and associated buildings are generally thought to be by James Miller, although the obituary of Robert Wemyss suggests he was responsible for the designs while working with J J Burnet.

Below *Station.*
Bottom *Taliesin West*

Rahane

curios in the grounds of the nearby coach-house, but it is the extraordinarily decorative bargeboards and finials, gable trefoils and intricate entrance porches which catch the eye.

CLYNDER
Until 1817, when the first feu of the Barremman Estate was taken up, the lee-side of the Rosneath peninsula was largely unpopulated. **Mambeg** and **Rahane**, two hamlets about a mile or so apart, grew quickly to their present size; one owing its existence to a small steamboat pier which closed in 1935, the other, at the foot of the **Mill Burn**, surviving in a row of whitewashed cottages on the shore road, including the now restored **Mill of Rahane**, an old ferryman's cottage and the ornately trimmed stone villa of **Aikenshaw**.

Clynder, derived from *Claon dearg*, meaning red slope, continues to expand, although with scant reference to the elegant villas first built at the foot of the bracken-clad braes. Despite the threat of further development, the village retains tangible attractions in its closeness to the water, its birdlife, and the magnificent, mature trees which stride along the shoreline.

Gareloch House, 1817
A gracious villa, symmetrical in undressed ashlar, with painted stone window surrounds, a low hipped roof and eaves cornice. To the rear is a little-known landscaped garden established in 1890. These beautifully arranged pleasure grounds formed part of the estate of **Achnashie**, the house to which the Revd John MacLeod Campbell retired in 1871. Like Achnashie, those parts of the garden outwith the policies of Gareloch House are derelict, but a rubble-walled **stables block** with arched screen walls survives among untamed clumps of rhododendrons beside the **Stroul Burn**.

North on the B833 a solitary drum-like gatepost announces the 1829 Regency mansion of **Stroul Lodge**. A broad, battlemented giant slumbering in greenery, it has twin bow-windows, huge gable chimney stacks, attendant wings and a Gothic porch to the side entrances of which a double curved staircase rises.

The commercial core of the village has been ripped out: McGruer's world-famous boatbuilding yard, which grew out of a single shed at the

Stroul Lodge

mouth of the **Hatton Burn**, has moved to
Rosneath (the old tin kirk which started life as a
Baptist Church and was transferred to
McGruer's works for use as a canteen, long since
abandoned), and the **Clynder Hotel** has burnt to
the ground. But some good farm buildings nestle
on the hillside, **Barremman** typically harled and
crow-stepped.

Glengair, *c*.1830

A single-storey symmetrical composition with
whitewashed wings, wide eaves and mullioned
and transomed windows. Adjoining two-storey
ranges create a large, sheltered courtyard.
Alongside is **Ardchoille**, 1901, recognisably
William Leiper, commissioned by George
MacGregor for his wife, Miss Thom of
Barremman. Leiper spurned the simplicity of
the local vernacular, reviving the red rosemary
tiled roof, half-timbered and tile-hung window
bays, and stone-clad staircase tower of his
upper Helensburgh villas.

ROSNEATH

No longer the *bare unwooded promontory* that
gave rise to the Gaelic *Rhosnoeth*, but a leafy
peninsula from which great vistas of the Firth
of Clyde are revealed: the uplands of
Renfrewshire, the slow wink of the Cloch
Lighthouse, the jaws of Loch Goil disgorging
into Loch Long, and the marine villas of the
larger Cowal peninsula to the west and the
Gareloch to the east.

Clynder

Below *Ardchoille*.
Bottom *Parish of Rosneath*

Rosneath Castle (*right*)
The original castle of the
Campbells of Argyll, whose
tenure as landowners began in
1489, was destroyed by fire in
1802 and replaced by John, 5th
Duke of Argyll, with a mansion,
1806, judged to be *the most
chaste and correct specimen of
its style in the kingdom*. The
style in question, while
betraying the Italian origins of
the architect, Joseph Bonomi
the Elder, was, more properly,
neoclassical – particularly the
great balustraded drum which
rose out of the roof above the
library. Additionally, the north
front, the only aspect of the
building completed, had an
unorthodox, elongated five-
columned Ionic *porte-cochère*
topped by a further balustrade.
These elements, combined with
the illusion of low horizontality,
worked to shape a ducal palace
whose elegance was unrivalled
in the West of Scotland. The
house remained unfinished and
was sold on the death of
Princess Louise, Dowager
Duchess of Argyll, in 1939.
After use as the administrative
centre for the American Naval
Base quartered at Rosneath
during the Second World War,
the building was abandoned to
be ignominiously blown up in
1961. All that can be seen today
is a caravan park sprawling
above the shores of **Camsail
Bay**.

Below right *Parkhead*.
Below *Bathwell*

Rosneath Home Farm, 1803,
Alexander Nasmyth (*below*)
A Gothick curiosity, three sides of an octagon
beneath a vast green envelope of corrugated tin.
Robbed of its steeple by fire, the central tower
aspires to a shabby grandeur, the doily effect of
the balustrade tracing patterns across the
skyline above the clutter of farm machinery.
Past the octagonal pavilions located on the
external knuckles of the building are round,
rendered bastions flanked by chubby turrets
and adorned with pointed blind windows.

Further north is **Parkhead**, originally the bothy
(now an architect's house), a splendid segmental
range coupled to a lovely sheltered, walled
garden. Close by, hidden in the forest, is classical
Bathwell, whose resemblance to the springhead
at Bealachanuaran at Inveraray suggests the
involvement of William Adam.

Clachan Village

A pretty, cloistered spot, steeped in antiquity, through which the **Clachan Burn** splashes past an avenue of ancient yews, the ruin of the old church and graveyard, and behind eight tiny cottages. Of these two are substantially rebuilt, none with the original thatched or red-tiled roofs, one formerly the smiddy and another the joiner's shop. The blacksmith's anvil remains, set down in front of the post office.

Clachan Village

St Modan's Parish Church, 1854,
David Cousin
Built to replace the second kirk of 1780, the ruinous south wall and ornate tiered bellcote of which still give sanctuary to a fascinating collection of obelisk-like gravestones. Enlarged by north and south transepts, 1862 and 1872, both with good stained-glass windows. Stocky, well buttressed and externally unpretentious St Modan's has an interesting interior; the 1610 Burgerhuis bell, which rang out in 1715 to call the parishioners to the first Jacobite rising, now rests inside. The reredos of the Last Supper, carved in oak by Meredith Williams, was gifted in 1931 by Princess Louise, in memory of her father-in-law and husband, the 8th and 9th Dukes respectively.

Below Old Parish Church and churchyard. Bottom St Modan's Parish Church

St Gilda's RC Church, 1968,
Thomas Cordiner
Acute, angular, the copper-clad roof scudding upwards to a point above a dramatic clerestory at the prow of which stands a tall cross. An arresting, if not slightly intimidating sight at the entrance to the village.

Ferry Inn, 1896-7, Edwin Lutyens
As if in anticipation of the inevitable
demolition of the hostelry for which it provided
enhanced bedrooms and ballroom, Lutyens's
now truncated wing of the Ferry Inn (built for
Princess Louise) is a complete architectural
statement; a little eclectic, not especially
Scottish, but as sympathetic to its now isolated
location as a private house on **Rosneath Point**
as it was to the original inn. The massing, from
the slightly battered variegated stone base to
the sweeping hipped roof and broad, arched
entrance porch, is Free Style. The minute,
metal-framed oriels tucked up beneath the
eaves are undoubtedly English, as is the
massive chimney performing geometric
acrobatics on the entrance front; but strength
and solidity give it a comforting, fortified
appearance, sited as it is on one of the most
exposed parts of the Gareloch. Years of use by
the American Navy led to the interior being
gutted; there are, however, two magnificent
back-to-back fireplaces in the living room and
kitchen, the two rooms linked by a lovely little
corridor backlit by the flickering light from
those very fires.

The whitewashed **Ferry Inn Cottage**
created out of the rear half of Lutyens's
extension to the inn has two jolly, slate-topped
exhaust stacks.

Ferry Inn

Dumbarton District Libraries

Sinclair

KILCREGGAN & COVE

Kilcreggan

Just as Kilcreggan and Cove owed their existence to the arrival of the steamship so its demise signalled an end to the development of the lower western fringe of the Rosneath peninsula. But inaccessibility has preserved architectural integrity; a narrow, winding shore road with snatches of breezy esplanade, lovely old lamp-standards whose glow is barely adequate at nightfall, cast-iron water pumps set by the road's edge, their lions' heads spouting into basins, and a long, leisurely row of villas and mansions of variety and stunning quality.

KILCREGGAN

Originally a series of small farms and cottages dependent on the ferry service linked to **Rosneath Inn**, Kilcreggan was developed on a more speculative basis than Cove. A pattern-book architecture emerged, a combination of steep gablets, rustic quoins, arched and dropped-arched windows, and decorative ironwork, all somehow transcending the ordinary; even the tenements on **Rosneath Road**, five big handsome blocks opposite the pier, built 1888 and 1903, have window dressings, gablets, strapwork and arches.

Uphill, on **Argyll Road**, is the **Kilcreggan Hotel** (formerly Woodvine), extended to the rear and west with some good stained-glass and ornate bargeboards, and a curious gabled and battlemented tower. Built by Robert Donaldson, whose brother erected the neighbouring mansion of Heathfield, now the **Kilcreggan Christian Conference Centre**. Below, **Aidenburn Cottage** is demure and decorative – open, looped bargeboards and a corbelled, extruded central porch.

Below *Water pump.* Bottom *Rosneath Road tenements*

Sinclair

Sinclair

Dunvronaig

Dunvronaig and **Dunvorleigh**,
Rosneath Road
Originally identical *cottage orné* villas, derived
in large part from Alexander Thomson's
Seymour Lodge in Cove (see p.113); enduring
red sandstone, blocky bays, Gothic drip-moulds
to the upper-floor windows, and the sensible
device of a small entrance porch with the door
turned from the sea. Roughly similar in
disposition are **Glenlea** and **Winton**, both
near **Craigrownie**, the latter still with its
whorling wrought-iron balustrade above the
living room bay. **Finnartmore** shares the side-
entry porch, but is broader with a full-height,
round bay and less decorative eaves.

Ardsloy, Rosneath Road
Delightful, dainty Greek-detailed villa
conceivably by Alexander Thomson, notably
slim (one room wide), and with an expansive
bow at ground floor, topped with an unusual
stone and iron balustrade. To the right is
Auchendarroch, big, Italianate, with tall,
scalloped indents at the corners and a lead
canopy tucked under the eaves.

Rosneath Road clings to the rocky, untamed
beach, a shoreline on which grass, moss and
clumps of daffodils manage to survive. Bathing
huts, the absence of which the author of the
Helensburgh Guide Book put down to the
slowness of *the Scotch mind to appropriate
ideas foreign to the groove in which ancestral
practice has worked*, would surely have been
impractical on Loch Long.
    Where a scrubby windbreak at last occurs
Claremont, **Lovedale**, **Holyrood** and
Aidenkyle have been built; all have faceted,
lead-roofed bays, pronounced quoins and
painted stonework. Aidenkyle has a little
lunette window high in the attic, and a
remarkably well-preserved cast-iron balustrade
linking entrance front to conservatory.

Former Kilcreggan Chapel

Balgair, Rosneath Road
Tripartite Italianate composition: gabled bay
with triple-arched upper-floor windows and
ornate balcony, and hipped wing with full-
height canted bay are linked together by a
low campanile with tiny square windows
lined up above a dentil course. Close by, near
the foot of **School Road**, **Glentrae** is very
much a kinsman of the earlier Ardsloy,
while **Lethington** is a traditional, sandstone

villa with lively arches over the upper windows. **Greenhill** has a pair of fine Glasgow Style gates.

School Road leads, not unexpectedly, to the stone-built **school** of 1867, complete with a shaped chimney, leaded, arched windows and good skew-puts and bellcote. Opposite is the harled symmetrical range of **Sunnyside Cottages** – windows dressed in yellow brick and ridge finished in yellow clay tiles.

CRAIGROWNIE

Kilcreggan is no longer served by either of the two churches built to accommodate the rapid increase in population: **Rosneath Free Church**, 1843, is a picturesque ruin next to the **Mill of Camsail** while the 1869 *iron church* built at the entrance to the village by Francis Morton of Liverpool, is now a garage.

Erected as a chapel of ease in 1852, **Craigrownie Parish Church**, enlarged by Honeyman & Keppie in 1889, alone remains to command spectacular views from its elevated site. John McElroy, an Irish mason who feued large parts of Cove, was responsible for drawing up the plans *with some help from a young Englishman*. The style is Early English Gothic, a steeply pitched roof on short, buttressed walls. There is a central bellcote above the chancel arch, a rose window on the west front, and two fussily detailed transepts, but the overall effect is good.

Craigrownie Church Hall, 1869,
Hugh Barclay
Two pairs of quite inappropriately voluptuous gateposts give entry to the grounds of this former U P Church. Successor to a wooden

Left *Craigrownie Parish Church*. Below *Craigrownie Church Hall*

Right *Burgh Hall & Reading Rooms*. Above *Signpost, Cove*

Cove Pier was built by John McElroy, a successful railway contractor, in collaboration with fellow developer Thomas Forgan. McElroy, retaining Alexander Thomson as principal architect, built along the shore road at Baron's Point, near Kilcreggan. From Thomson's work the area has derived its marked character; those who followed – such as Hugh Barclay and, possibly, James Boucher – could scarcely fail to be inspired by the beautiful shores, the local materials (in particular, the quartz which littered the beaches) and Thomson's example.

Thomson's last recorded works on the peninsula were sponsored by the publisher Robert Blackie, who commissioned a magnificent pair of garden gates for **Ferndean Villa** in 1863 (see p.113), and headed the committee who appointed Thomson to design a small shore bridge at the foot of **Dowall Burn** in 1874.

Glen Eden

building erected on the site in 1858, it is a lofty barn-like structure, cruciform in plan and patterned with a flagstone effect.

Cove Burgh Hall & Reading Rooms, Rosneath Road, 1893
Scots Renaissance, rubble-built with red sandstone dressings and details; slightly incongruous with its bright red clay-tiled roof and municipal heartiness. The recreation rooms are located on the left with the library above, linked to a wide-arched entrance front with armorial carvings by a conical roofed tower containing a subsidiary entrance and highlighted by a corbelled, carved, much elongated dormer. Opposite, on a lovely grassy resting place above the shore, is the town's **War Memorial**.

COVE
In sight of the villas of **Strone** and **Blairmore** (see pp.135-7) and the glowering heights of the **Argyll Forests**, a lengthy spinal cliff encrusted with the wealth of industrialists and entrepreneurs provides the architectural highpoint of the promontory. Above the rugged beauty of a boulder-strewn beach, great *bouffants* of greenery mask the sides of the ridge. From the twin peaks which define the curve of **Cove Bay**, **Cove Castle** and **Knockderry Castle** eye one another imperiously.

Kirklea, Rosneath Road
An unconventional, acute, square-cut gabled front with a shallow splayed bedroom bay – full height windows opening up behind a cast-iron balustrade. Next door, resplendent in its woodland garden is **Glen Eden**, *c.*1851, a highly ornate Italianate design with whinstone-relieving arches, a complex shallow

roofscape, chunky corbels and an unusual bowed extension to the rear. Best of all are the blocky quartz gateposts.

Craigrownie Castle, South Ailey Road, *c*.1854, Alexander Thomson
An extensive Scots Baronial pile rising up from the foot of the hillside on a battered stone base; crisply detailed with receding gables on the garden front. There are two huge canted and corbelled oriels, and a high, square battlemented turret reduced to a more humane scale on the entrance elevation. Opposite, three needle obelisks sit on the gatepiers of Campbell Douglas's demolished Hartfield House, 1859.

Craigrownie Castle

Craig Ailey, South Ailey Road, 1850, Alexander Thomson
One of Thomson's earliest known designs, a summer residence built for John McElroy; eloquent Italian with a marked Germanic neoclassical accent, notably in the use of the campanile as a compositional device. From the striated stone podium whose random masonry mimics the cliff-face on which it sits, to the flattened pyramidal cap of the belvedere, this picturesque villa stretches up to enjoy the scenic expanse of the Firth of Clyde. In the semicircular drawing-room window, one of the

Craig Ailey, Kilcreggan, from Villa & Cottage Architecture, 1868

first uses of patent rolled plate glass; in the shallow protruding eaves and (now missing) Greek ornament, tentative indications of the style in which Thomson was to excel. The gateposts, slender freestone with indents of quartz, share the corbels, shallow headgear and peeping eyes of the staircase tower.

Thomson's boundary wall to Craigrownie Castle, crosses of wrought-iron recurring in rhythms of threes and fours, encloses the ground at the base of the cliff, being interrupted at **Craigrownie Cottage** by two portly conch-like piers. Dating back to 1837, the cottage is much recast, but fresh and attractive with a quartz-studded central gable with shapely curves below the eaves.

Right *Crag Owlet Cottages.* Below *Cove Village.* Middle *Clevedon Hotel / The Towers.* Bottom *Cove Castle*

Crag Owlet Cottages, Rosneath Road
In the shadow of the burnt-out shell of **Baron Cliff**, stand four houses disguised as an elaborate, symmetrical tenement, a ghoulish amalgam of exaggerated Scots Gothic, jaggedly responsive to the rugged site. Protruding gabled wings, with scalloped bays and stubby porches, are linked together above a battered, schistose base by a slated canopy, and dotted with tiny, tripartite openings and heraldic plaques.

Past the village shops the house of **Claremont** glowers fiercely from the entangled slopes below **North Ailey Road**, and the frothy confection of the **Clevedon Hotel** serves only to emphasise the gaunt ruin of **The Towers** behind.

Cove Castle, 1867, James Sellars
Lovely, diminutive castle set high above an immaculate lawn. The inner turret has elliptical openings which recur on the south-

west bastion; there is a slender, corbelled oriel to the drawing room, and a cast-iron balustrade in lieu of battlements.

Cove Pier subsists as two stumps of timber rotting in the clutches of wave-lashed rocks. Opposite, **Ashlea** and **Ellerslie**, twin gabled houses linked by a stone veranda, served as the

Seymour Lodge from Villa & Cottage Architecture, *1868*

local hotel. Nearby is **Seymour Lodge**, 1850, Alexander Thomson, a perky seaside villa peeping up to sniff the sea air, its *cottage orné* idiom inspiring a host of similar houses along the water's edge. The architect's original elaborate decoration is now confined to the crocketed ridges and balustrade above the dining-room bay.

An exceptionally high standard of design is maintained as the feus grow more northerly; the smaller villas such as **Burncliff Cottage**, **Strathlee** and **Birken Hillock** are in the main indebted to Seymour Lodge. Others are larger and round-arched, **Grafton** with flattened gablets, **Brookvale** with bulky corbels on pilasters, and **Lucerne** with a lacy balcony and oversailing eaves. **The Linn**, 1858, William Motherwell, an extruded Italianate mansion perched above the **Meikle Waterfall**, is the fledgeling sister of Craig Ailey, the family resemblance striking. At **Deeplands**, now a retirement home, rustic quoins, eaves dripping with ornament, and a distinctive neoclassical pavilion.

Woodside is Edwardian with a good pyramid-topped tower, and the Cove-Gothic clutter of **Cragdarroch**, once owned by the Teacher family of distillers, is lively and unusual. **Glen Holly**, whose twin at **Glen Rowan** is paler complexioned, is finely ordered with a frilly bracketed barrel porch on slender posts.

Below *The Linn*. Bottom *Gates to Ferndean Villa from* Villa & Cottage Architecture, *1868*

Knockderry Castle

Mitchell Library

Knockderry Castle, 1855, John Honeyman?
Said to have been built on the dungeons of an
ancient Danish or Norwegian lookout tower
(dating probably from about the time of the
Battle of Largs), Knockderry is magnificently
poised at the edge of a rocky outcrop, organically
allied to the cliff below and spectacularly
enlarged to the rear in 1896 by William Leiper.
Its bulk, barely lifted by a serrated skyline, gives
little hint of the delightful interior wherein can
be found a water-powered lift (installed for carpet
manufacturer and weaver John S Templeton),
and a glorious banqueting hall in blue and gold,
complete with minstrels' gallery and frieze.

Leiper's lighthearted alterations to
Knockderry House Hotel date from the same
period. Here, ubiquitous half-timbering on the
upper and attic storeys, blonde sandstone bays,
an asymmetrical central portion where Old
English fairly shoulders out Old Scots, and a
squat octagonal wing to the north on which
three spikey dormers jostle for room.

Knockderry House Hotel

Dick

Further north, **Bellcairn** is fast deteriorating,
while **Auchengower** – the banded,
battlemented entrance tower ill-matched to the
steep piended roof and assortment of bays and
bows – is surrounded by a caravan park. But
their lodges remain, albeit in altered form, that
to Bellcairn with Egypto-Greek chimney pots
and Dalek-like gatepiers, the other jaggedly
Scots Gothic with lozenge and fishscale slates,
a splayed bay and two-tier timbered gable.
Curving protectively around the two is a
splendid cast-iron railing, the decoration dying
as Coulport comes into view.

COULPORT

Notable less for what survives than for what has been destroyed in defence of the realm; there is an old tin kirk and some two-storey sandstone villas but the damage wreaked on the landscape by the Royal Naval Armaments Depot is awesome.

Lost in the clearance of the 1960s was John Kibble's **Coulport House**, *c*.1860, James Boucher, a good Italianate mansion with campanile, round-headed windows with pilasters and touches of elegant ironwork. Of the two conservatories associated with the house, the larger – built reputedly at a cost of £15,000 – was donated to Glasgow's Botanic Gardens, being towed upriver in 1872 and re-erected with the addition of a huge dome.

Boucher's own house, built alongside and also demolished, could not have been more different: a Swiss chalet complete with timber shutters, a stencil-traced balcony hugging the first-floor level, and delicate brackets and bargeboards.

Peaton House, early 19th century
The curvaceous gable end of a stone barn on the **Peaton Road** to the Gareloch leads the eye round to the farmhouse proper, two storeys and attic with limewashed and harled façades extending out to the east in a small, piended wing, and rising up through extruded dormers – the central window a tiny triangle.

FINNART

From Coulport the newly completed Garelochhead Bypass effects a slick swathe across the promontory, pausing briefly at the junction with Whistlefield before descending to Faslane. For the breathtaking views of the Gareloch one is almost prepared to forgive the intrusive ribbon of tarmac, the newness of it all soon forgotten as the A814 scrambles on its well-worn path to the head of Loch Long.

Top *Swiss Villa, Coulport House & Kibble Palace*. Middle *Conservatory (not Kibble Palace)*. Above *Mr James Boucher*

John Kibble, photographer, astronomer, botanist and greenhouse constructor, died at Coulport House in 1894. He is best remembered for the Kibble Palace, the lovely glass and iron conservatory which he offered first to Queen's Park in Glasgow and, later, to the Botanic Gardens. Kibble retained the right to hold concerts and other functions in the glasshouse, agreeing that of any profits raised, £930 should go to the Royal Botanic Institution, with the next £300 to himself. Removal of the building to Glasgow was a blessing indeed; it would likely have perished had it remained at Loch Long.

Whistlefield and Loch Goil

Sinclair

Through **Whistlefield**, past an outsize green kettle whose spout gestures to the whitewashed inn opposite, the old drovers' road drops to **Portincaple**. Important as a marshalling point for cattle swum in from Argyll – this before the military road from Dumbarton to Inveraray was completed in 1768 – the village clings to the romance of its past in roofless ruins of stables and pens. No such threads of tradition, however, cling to **Dalriada**, 1909, Watson & Salmond, a red-pantiled bungalow swelling out above the village road – white walls, shaped chimneys, a horseshoe-shaped veranda and a bulbous attic window staring unblinkingly out over Loch Goil. Also in the village, on the shore, the Arts & Crafts cottage of **Inveralit**, 1900, Eric Sutherland.

Above *Green Kettle at Whistlefield*. Right *Dalriada, Portincaple*

Sinclair

At **Finnart**, the *fair, beautiful headland* marking the boundary between Highlands and Lowlands, John, Duke of Argyll, erected a tablet commemorating the 1787 construction of the road from Rosneath to Arrochar. To this magnificent wooded shore later came British Petroleum, opening their first deepwater terminal there in 1951, built to accommodate tankers bringing crude oil from the Middle East, then piped 57 miles underground to Grangemouth Refinery.

ARROCHAR

Ardarroch House, 1838, William Burn, Enlarged by David Bryce in 1847 and now staff quarters for BP Finnart, Ardarroch has a courteous, almost diffident air; fleeting excitement created by the unusual frequency of the chimney stacks. Some years earlier Burn had evolved the prototype at **Finnart House** opposite, a two-storey villa with lower ancillary wing and concave curves to the upper bays. On the road's edge is Ardarroch **East Lodge**, single storey with a big splayed bay, perilously close to the burn adjacent. Upriver, **Finnart Lodge** cares less about wet feet; a lovely, round building with conical roof – single storey with a porch on the bridge side and a precipitous two storeys falling into the burn below at the rear.

Left *Ardarroch House.*
Above *Finnart Lodge*

ARROCHAR

The most northerly parish in the county of Dunbarton, Arrochar left Robert Burns singularly unimpressed: *a land of savage hills, swept by savage rains, peopled by savage sheep, tended by savage people* he wrote, his opinion no doubt coloured by the legendary wrongdoings of the local lairds, the lawless, cattle-thieving MacFarlanes. Writing in the 1790 Statistical Account, the Revd John Gillespie was inclined to agree that the population were prone to *misanthropy and ferocity of manners*, but in their favour they had *a strong attachment to the laird as chief*.

The highest peaks – **Ben Vorlich**, **Ben Vane**, **Ben Ime** and **Ben Arthur** (The Cobbler) – are unfailingly attractive to hillwalkers, while the locals peaceably eke out a living from forestry and tourism, and the sheep graze indolently among the gravestones grouped around the **Parish Church**, 1847.

The ruins of the first church, an arched entranceway, two round openings and a blind doorway, lie to the south of the churchyard. Although bound in 1648 to erect a kirk, manse

Loch Long
While the Loch Lomondside road to Tarbet bears the fresh scars of progress, the route from Finnart to Arrochar remains largely unchanged from when horse and carriage provided the principal mode of transport: along the route some good whitewashed cottages, several roofless but'n'bens, and great spreads of *rhododendron ponticum* which threaten to narrow the already sparse passage. Half-way up the loch, past the incongruous sight of four stalky cranes wheelbound on a pier, the entrance to **Glen Douglas**, its serene beauty unruffled by the huge ammunition silos buried there since 1956.

The road along Loch Long to Arrochar, c.1900

and glebe, the MacFarlanes had continued to cross the isthmus to Luss until 1733, when the church there was finally judged to be inadequate for the combined parishes. The present church, roughcast with a good central tower with louvred belfry and pretty Gothic pinnacles, is a worthy successor to the role.

Ardmay House, 1853

On the shores of Loch Long, now a retirement home for the elderly, the gracious stone-built mansion of Ardmay. Extended for William Black in 1922 by A N Paterson, who appears to have added the timbered porch and conical-roofed south tower. There is a good organ in the entrance hall.

Inveriach House, c.1785

Inveriach (or Arrochar) House, reconstructed by Ferguson of Raith on purchase of the parish, has harled walls and scrolled skew-puts, but the sturdy detailing has survived better on a nearby single-storey cottage. The 1776 **Steadings**, a U-shaped courtyard range converted to private housing, retains ball finials to the gable ends and moulded entablatures to two of the original doorways. Nearby, the **Cobbler Hotel**, symmetrical blonde sandstone with ebullient bargeboards and dormers, bears a lintel engraved with the 1697 date of the clan chief's Arrochar seat.

Top *Parish Church.*
Above *Ardmay House*

In 1742, the Honourable Helen Arbuthnot bequeathed the sum of 200 Scots merks to buy a bell for the parish kirk of **Arrochar**. Years elapsed before the bell was finally acquired and, as there was no place for it on the old church, it was hung on a bell-tree in the grounds. Apparently, one Malcolm MacFarlane, having been summoned to the Kirk Session and reprimanded for some misdemeanour, left the manse in an angry mood. Passing the bell he thought first of pulling on it to relieve his annoyance, but instead, on spying a neighbour's goat, tethered the unfortunate creature to the bell and left it struggling to escape. *Out came Minister and Session to seek the cause. Seeing an uncanny-looking thing with horns rushing to and fro in the twilight, some of the Session thought it was Auld Nick himself, and it was only when the Minister mustered up courage enough to approach the tree that he found it was old Mary Campbell's goat.* The bell now resides in the belfry of the present church, none the worse for its adventures.

In line with its popularity as a stopping-off place *en route* to Inveraray, Arrochar is plentifully endowed with boarding houses and hotels: **Arrochar Hotel** (*below*), A N Paterson, has suffered an identity crisis, the original Scots vernacular no longer able to hold its own alongside mediocre modern enlargements, but

Lynwood Hotel, 1837 (formerly the manse), is much better, white harling against which window margins, quoins and moulded boxed eaves are picked out in black. Nearby, **Mansefield**, *c*.1880, is more ornate, dark grey masonry with toothy yellow dressings at windows and quoins, a pedimented entranceway and loosely looped bargeboards.

Arrochar from the pier, c.1900

Other large houses, such as the gabled Tudor box of **Benreoch** surprise by their complexity, but it is the council and Admiralty-built housing at Tighness which has succeeded to the diminutive scale of the original thatched cottages. **Kirkfield Place**, 1938, Joseph

Kirkfield Place

Weekes, is delightful – three sides of a square, symmetrical about a pend, with a sinuous, slated roof – rising here to a gablet, dipping there into a mansard, shrouded always in lazy spirals of smoke. The mansards are broadened and trimmed in red on the **Admiralty Cottages** (built in 1939 to house workers at the now defunct torpedo range opposite), while the gablets are steepened in the asymmetrical semi-detached houses on **Cobbler View**, *c*.1950.

The village is less distinctive towards the head of the loch; the **Church of St Peter & Paul**, 1953, Jack Coia, is scarcely distinguished by the blocky stone entrance-cum-belfry, but the house of **Glenloin**, hidden in a caravan park, comes as a pleasant surprise – a shallow, Ionic-columned porch at the centre of severe classical symmetry.

Top *Church of St Peter & Paul.*
Above *Arrochar from the north-east, c.1900*

Tighvechtichan & Ballyhennan

Just as Loch Long and the Gareloch are barely separated at Garelochhead, Tarbet and Arrochar are but two-and-a-half miles apart. While the 1821 canal, designed by engineer James Baird to link Loch Long and Loch Lomond, failed to materialise, there are the remains of General Wade's earlier crossing, and the more effortless passage of the West Highland Railway.

At Tighvechtichan, half-way to Loch Lomondside, the MacFarlanes had their watchtower to levy blackmail on all traffic passing along the drovers' road. Nearby, adjacent to **Arrochar & Tarbet Station** – Swiss-style like its sole-surviving mate at Garelochhead (see p.101) – is **Arrochar Free Church**, 1844, plain but with an unexpectedly large steeple, and given new hope as an **arts & crafts centre** after years of misuse as a garage. Behind, is the **Ballyhennan Burying Ground**, where the bodies of the plundering Norse Vikings of 1263 are buried.

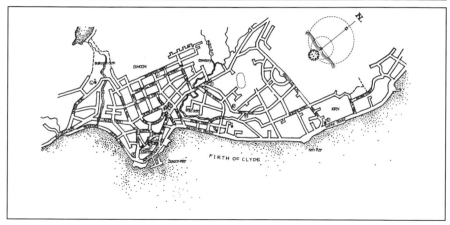

DUNOON CASTLE & PIER

Dunoon Castle, 14th century
Pushing out into the Firth between East Bay
and West Bay, Castle Hill is the obvious site
for a defensive stronghold on the east coast of
Cowal. The Castle itself is, however, less easy
to see. All that remains is a rough outcrop of
fragmentary foundation; no sign of the three-
towered Royal palace referred to by Jamieson
in his *Select Views of the Royal Palaces of
Scotland* (1840).

Dunoon Castle

   The skyline of Castle Hill is today marked by
craggy vestiges of the old foundations, a
flagpole, a direction indicator, and the bronze
figure of D W Stevenson's *Highland Mary*,
1896 – ill-fated, Burns's love looks wanly out
across the Firth towards Kyle.

A **Castle Buildings**, 1822, David Hamilton
Castle House was erected by the Lord Provost
of Glasgow, James Ewing, whose attraction to
the site led him to carry out some early
antiquarian researches on the old castle and
may have influenced his decision to
commission Hamilton's *marine villa* in the
castellated Gothic style. Full of crenellations,
hood-mouldings and four-centred arches, the
house seemed *as if sprung from the ruins of the
scarce discernible walls of the ancient fortalice.*

Castle Buildings

   In 1893 the property was bought by the Town
Council and it remains in local authority
hands, functioning today as the **Tulloch
Library**. There is a **gate-house**, mid 19th
century, in the same Gothic idiom and a fine
rubble wall, *c*.1835, with which Ewing enclosed
most, but not all, of his estate grounds.

Dunoon was Lamont land, though the earliest castle probably passed into royal ownership in the 12th century following the marriage of Walter Fitzalan, High Steward of Scotland, into the Lamont family. In the 14th century the Stewarts rebuilt the castle – an event which, it has been suggested, may account for the name Dunoon, i.e. *new castle*. The Campbells of Argyll were made hereditary keepers, acquired the lordship of Cowal in 1471-2 and, despite their temporary loss of the castle during the Earl of Lennox's revolt in 1544, continued to keep possession of Dunoon. From the 17th century, however, the Campbells lived at Inveraray and Dunoon Castle fell into disrepair and ruin: in 1883 Inglis's guide reported it *a complete wreck, due to the ravages of Time and the abstraction of stones by the villagers for building purposes.*

In 1835, James Ewing began to build a wall around his Dunoon demesne. The villagers, angered at the restrictions thus imposed on their access to Castle Hill, began to demolish Ewing's wall. Each night a small group, in which the local women were apparently prominent, would dismantle the stonework constructed during the previous day. The local laird, MacArthur Moir, who had granted Ewing his feu charter, sided with the protesters.

Ewing asserted what he believed to be his rights and the accused villagers were taken to the Court at Inveraray. There, however, Ewing's actions were deemed unlawful, the Dunoon demolishers were exonerated and the wall remained incomplete.

Along with the contemporary mansions of Castle Toward (see p.141) and Hafton House (see p.130), Castle House set an architectural fashion for later villa building on the Cowal shore; from Toward Point to Holy Loch, romantic forms found favour.

Dunoon Pier (*below*), 1896-8, Clarke & Bell The first pier was erected in 1835 but frequent paddle-steamer traffic needed better facilities and in 1867 Mr Hunter of Hafton House had a larger pier and waiting room built. In 1881 this, in turn, was improved so that the jetty extended almost 400ft from the shore. Fifteen years later the construction of the present two-berth pier was begun.

To the north is a symmetrical gabled-and-bayed building from the centre of which emerges an octagonal lounge, its roof rising to an ogee-capped clock; on the south, a pagoda-like signalling tower now joined to later less imaginative additions. Red-tiled roofs and strongly detailed timber colourfully rehabilitated, 1980-1, Strathclyde Region Architects, in chocolate, cream and yellow. A promenade balcony erected in 1937 has not been renewed, though the much-altered entrance buildings from the Pier Esplanade do remain.

Dunoon Town Centre
When Ewing built his *castle* in 1822, Dunoon was no more than *a small Highland township*, a few cottages clustered around the village church. None of these early dwellings remains but something of the spirit of the place does survive in the organic plan of the streets climbing around the hill behind Castle Buildings. Georgian in architectural character, **Kirk Street** nonetheless preserves this more ancient sense of village containment.

Several early 19th-century buildings reinforce the old townscape: **44** Kirk Street, a plain three-bay house with square dressings and quoins; **Ballochyle House**, similar but skew gabled, and **Glasgow Hotel**, c.1850, piended with a consoled eaves. A later tall three-storey tenement at **26-28** Kirk Street, made even taller by its high gabled attic dormers, has been rehabilitated by McGurn, Logan, Duncan & Opfer. The wide north transept of the parish kirk completes the sense of enclosure while good rubble walls, binding all the elements together, run along Kirk Street and down Kirk Brae by the graveyard to the Castle Gardens.

B **Old Parish Church**, from 1816, J Gillespie Graham
Gillespie Graham's Late Decorated Gothic Revival church was lengthened in 1834 by Ewing's architect David Hamilton. But it is width not length which impresses – in the west front with its traceried windows and trefoil light, and in the double-bay transepts, 1909, by Andrew Balfour. Crenellated parapets enclose the roof and there are crocketed finials on every buttress. A square belfry tower, raised in 1839, projects at the east.

Top *44 Kirk Street.*
Above *Old Parish Church*

King Street's enclave of late Georgian buildings continues in **2-20**, a rehabilitated skew-gabled terrace with two pilastered doorpieces. In an aberrant corner of polychromatic brick a bold semicircular window looks down Ferry Brae. Gable-to-gable shops and housing border **Hillfoot Street** where **28** has an attractive bay corbelled on a bulbous ogee over a pend and **18** has acquired three barrel dormers similar to those on the Argyll Hotel (see p.124).

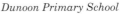

Dunoon Primary School

C William Fraser's **Dunoon Primary School**, c.1907, formerly Dunoon Grammar School, produces an abrupt change: a chequered mass of windows and quoining with a bartizaned tower, some Gothic tracery and, most unusual, vesical glazing to the doors in the arched entrance way.

Milton Avenue opens out, edging towards the more residential uptown streets that begin at **Royal Crescent**. A small but busy Gothic mansion, converted in 1967 to **District Council Offices** but still preserving its original horizontally proportioned glass panes, marks the transition west into villa-land.

Right *Caledonian Hotel.*
Below *67 Argyll Street*

Before the Queen's Hall was built, **Dunoon** had its less grandly named but more joyfully designed **Public Pavilion**. Erected between 1903 and 1905 on exactly the same site, it too provided a large concert hall, café, terraces and other holiday facilities. There was an open-air bandstand and pert pagoda-roof portals opening from the promenade. The architect, William Fraser, contrived a concoction of Arts & Crafts forms organised around a central swept-eaves dome.

Argyll Hotel

Ferry Brae, on the other hand, still strongly streetwise, curves downhill into town. The dormered, black-and-white wall of the **Caledonian Hotel**, 1903, William Fraser, makes a slow powerful bend into Argyll Street. Incorporated in its façade are some original shopfronts bound together by the strong horizontals of stringcourses and parapet above. At **67 Argyll Street**, a three-storey gushet dramatises another original shopfront, 1858. **Argyll Street** is Dunoon's main street. It

D starts back at Castle Gardens with considerable ambition where **Queen's Hall**, 1956-8, Ninian Johnston, with seats for a thousand, is an enthusiastic farrago of 1950s fashion. Big and ungainly but festively variegated in materials, both theatre foyer and restaurant fully glazed for panoramic views of the Clyde, its seaside vulgarity seems somehow almost ready for sympathetic re-evaluation.

Street front bulk is more orthodoxly sustained by **No 35** Argyll Street, 1894, David V Wyllie, a wide four-storey tenement with gabled dormers, and, in lower key, by **Crown Buildings**, 1905, John Breingan, with its unusual upper storey of round-arched leaded lights. But the earliest and still the most effective rise in scale comes, across the street,

E at the **Argyll Hotel**. Begun *c*.1850 as a three-storey piended block above the rocks, its original Grecian entrance-way suggests the hand of Alexander Thomson. In 1876 a new entrance was made through an Ionic porch at the base of a tall campanile-like tower, barrel dormers were introduced along the old roof and, after the creation of the esplanade leading into East Bay, a low convex balconied wing with five glazed arches was added in 1909 by D Andrew.

Beyond the Argyll Hotel, the street is two-sided and, in the main, two-storeyed. **No 82**, *c*.1860 (?), Peddie & Kinnear, is an exception –

higher, gabled and round-arched, with pink Buchan granite columns fronting a recessed timber entrance screen – for generally the mood is, or was, quietly classical. There is coherence but little quality, though a few sandstone houses hold on to their architectural dignity above the commercialisation at pavement level.

F **St Cuthbert's Church**, 1875, Clarke & Bell
In a high, richly carved gable front, Decorated windows soar above an eight-light arcade; to the right, a stair tower, impressive enough even without the steeple that would have dominated Church Street. The drama comes from the steep hillside site, but the entrance façade on Albert Crescent, though less tall, is equally lavish in detail.

St Cuthbert's Chuch

Burgh Buildings, 1873-4, Robert A Bryden
In the same grey-green random rubble as the church alongside, its windowed gable facing Argyll Street is church-like too. But the spirit is secular: Baronial, not Gothic.

Below *Burgh Buildings*.
Bottom *St John's Church*

G **St John's Church**, 1876-7, Robert A Bryden
A magnificent nave-and-aisles kirk, with five traceried gablets to each aisle, built to supersede the Free Church of 1843. Halls on Victoria Road detract a little from the rose window and flanking towers of the west end but the church is splendidly sited on Hanover Street, a Normandy Gothic spired tower at the east pointing up its elevation above the town. The galleried concert hall interior has plaster-ribbed ceilings.

Argyll Street continues to run northwards out of the centre of town. A smart tenement at **53-61 John Street**, 1910, four storeys of ashlar accentuating a bay-windowed corner in pudding basin dome, is almost the last piece of urban streetscape. Thereafter the scale drops.
H Wholly domestic, the former **Police Station**, 1870, J C Walker, at the corner of Argyll Road, is in Scots vernacular revival style – a typically disposed L-plan completed by a cone-roofed turnpike stair in the re-entrant angle. The new **Police Headquarters**, 1975, by Argyll County Architects Department, are no taller but white walls, flat roofs and ribbon windows impart an efficient if less humane aura to authority. Flatted housing at **1-58 Queen Street** is comparably institutional though the

Marshall Court

Dick

incongruity of its four- and five-storey bulk is mitigated by tile-hung walls and glazed gallery links. Regrettably, the landscaping is harsh and unimaginative. Sheltered housing at **Marshall Court**, 1978, Thomas Smith, Gibb & Pate, makes a much better job of it.

UPPER TOWN
Uphill, suburban Dunoon takes the form of an imperfect rectilineal grid of streets. The layout, and most of the houses – terraces, villas and cottages – date from the last quarter of the 19th century. There is little consistency, but here and there details catch the eye: a bowed shopfront uniting **129-131 Edward Street** with **127-131 John Street**; a concave corbel over a chamfered corner at **Woodside**, Mary Street; the rounded corners and nautical railings of **Carradale**, *c.*1938, also on Mary Street; floral leaded glass in pink and violet at **81 Edward Street**; a lovely fretted eaves line at **Lin Mar**, **52 McArthur Street**, ill respected by crass dormers. Many two-storey properties are flatted, with open spiralling stairs at the rear; at **Firth View**, on Alexander Street, for example, these stairs are enclosed in curving glazed tubes that seem to derive from Edwardian railway architecture.

Below *Firth View*.
Bottom *Auchamore House*

Dick

Auchamore House, *c.*1830
Originally a courtyard farm, its rubble walls are rugged and plain, the house itself standard three-bay Georgian with a Roman Doric pilastered doorpiece. From here **Auchamore Road** dips into the valley of the **Balgie Burn** and **Bishop's Glen**, while to the north the long straight line of **Alexander Street**, marking the edge of town, extends as far as the tired pavilions of W G Rowan's **Fever Hospital**, 1897, sitting beside the cemetery above **Milton Burn**.

RCAHMS

RCAHMS

WEST BAY

South of the pier, traffic avoids the West Bay
shore by way of **Tom-a-Mhoid Road**, a peaked
K pyramid on the **Cosy Corner Tearoom**
marking the change of direction jauntily. On
the edge of Castle Gardens, is the **Lamont
Memorial**, 1906, a Celtic cross cut in a granite
dolmen to commemorate the clan's l7th-century
sufferings at the hands of the Campbells.
Rosegarth Hotel clings desperately to an
ambience of friendly Gothick compromised by
the smooth white-walled mass of its neighbour,
McColl's Hotel, 1938, A MacGregor Mitchell.

The walk from Castle Hill along West Bay
passes **Englemere**, an oddly English mixture
with wide canted bays, and then reaches a long
esplanade terrace whose dormered mansard
roof stretches from the raised attics of **Milton
Tower** to those of the **West End Hotel**.
Esplanade Hotel, 1908, also bulges with
tiered bays as does **Abbot's Brae Hotel**,
though it has a more composed symmetrical
elegance and its site, perched in the trees
above the bay, is more secluded. Similarly
favoured in location, **Ardfillayne Hotel**, 1835,
is a chimneyed, crow-stepped mansion in
unrestrained Gothick. More controlled in form,
3-47 Bullwood Road follow the shore south in
an orderly series of semi-detached villas, their
broad bays crested with decorative ironwork.

Dick

Dick

Top *West Bay.* Middle *Cosy
Corner Tearoom.* Above
McColl's Hotel

L **Holy Trinity Church**, 1850, John Henderson
Set apart on Kilbride Hill in wooded
landscaped grounds, this simple Gothic Revival
church is cast in familiar nave-and-chancel
mould. The pattern is pleasantly augmented,
however, by a slated crenellated tower on the
south-east and a memorial chapel, 1896, by the
Inverness architect Alexander Ross at the rear
of the nave. In an interior of roughly plastered
walls and open timber roof, the oddest touch is
a stairway to the pulpit *tunnelled* through the
chancel arch.

Holy Trinity Church

Dick

Top *Clyde Cottage*. Middle *Argyll House*. Above *Coach houses*

EAST BAY

Of the buildings that fill the sea front from the Argyll Hotel (see p.124) to the Swimming Pool, 1968, the less said the better, for nothing responds to the privilege of the esplanade. Only the recent **Tourist Information Office** is tidy and trim; but it makes nothing of its seaside opportunity.

At **Alexandra Parade** architectural dignity begins to return, though the necklace of older houses along the bay is erratically sized and not a little tarnished. First in line and quality is **Clyde Cottage**, *c*.1830, its pedimented Ionic doorway entered up an iron-railed rising stair. **Tigh-Na-Mara** sports a slender-shafted broken-pedimented porch. Much more severe and urbane, **Victoria Terrace**, *c*.1850, stretches out between canted ground-floor bays that have tripartite windows above. **Argyll House**, 1908, is abruptly tall but worth something for its ironwork veranda.

Behind the esplanade runs **George Street**, older, lower and altogether more *towny*. There are several simple single-storey properties, some of the best round a concave corbelled corner at **3-9 Milton Road**, bricked-up windows blinding it to the view of the Firth down Nile Street.

Some distance up the hill on Argyll Road, two properties merit mention. Through the roadside wall of a former mansion's **coach-houses**, *c*.1840, a four-centred arch leads to a cobbled courtyard from which outside stairs rise to upper flats. Though rehabilitated, hood-mouldings and blind loopholes recall the medievalist fashion of the day. **Edgemont**, *c*.1938, on the other hand, at **34 Argyll Road**, is a squat flat-roofed villa of the 1930s, modishly Moderne, with ship-railed balconies and chevron opening lights.

Edgemont

KIRN

By 1845 Kirn had a pier of its own, as sure a
sign of its increasing sense of independence
from Dunoon as its more salubrious residences
and hotels. In 1893 it completed its esplanade
and the following year plans for a Pavilion
were prepared but never realised. The twin-
drummed brick pierhead buildings, 1895, H E
Clifford, have gone, but villas and hotels still
abound. Along the Parade, **Ashgrove** is a
piled-up mass of Gothick with open eaves and
bargeboarded gables; **Rosemount**, trimmed in
lacy ironwork, is symmetrically stressed by its
central Italianate tower; while **Queen's Hotel**,
1905, Boston, Menzies & Morton, opposite the
pier, is a fascinating collage of Arts & Crafts
tricks: half-timbering, stone and roughcast;
balconies, verandas and gables; a corbelled
corner tower.

Above *Queen's Hotel.*
Left *Kirn Parish Church*

O **Kirn Parish Church**, 1906-7,
P MacGregor Chalmers
A subtly and beautifully sited church in red
rock-faced sandstone Romanesque. There is a
single gabled transept, three half-coned apses
at the east end and a four-stage belfry tower
capped by a steep stone pyramid: the
composition and the carving are of the highest
quality. Reserved and impeccably judged, this
may well be the finest piece of architecture on
the whole Cowal shore.

Kirn Brae climbs uphill from the church in a
tenemented curve, crosses Hunter Street and
continues east as Ardenslate Road. Three older
properties offer something special. **Shuna
Lodge** presents a full-width pilastered porch
reprehensibly roofed in corrugated iron; at **16
Ardenslate Road** the porch, semicircular in

Royal Marine Hotel

projection, is both pillared and pilastered; while at **Kirn & Hunter's Quay Bowling Club**, the mood is increasingly classical for here, below a piended roof, is an elegantly proportioned eight-bay Roman Doric loggia.

HUNTER'S QUAY

In 1828 the laird of Hafton Estate, Robert Hunter, built a stone quay not only for the convenience of his own new home, Hafton House, which he had built to overlook the approaches of Holy Loch, but with a view to stimulating further residential and leisure development in the area. His enterprise was successful: the wealthy came, mansions and hotels were built, and Hunter's Quay became a mecca for Clyde yachtsmen.

It was the **Royal Marine Hotel**, 1888, built by T L Watson for his boat-building brother, which became the headquarters of the Royal Northern (later Royal Clyde) Yacht Club. It looks less than nautical – more like a great Tudor hall from deep in the English shires with a parapeted stone tower thrown in for good measure. Its well-windowed, gable-crested façade is a magnificent sight and a reminder of the Clyde's great days of steam and sail.

Hafton House, 1816, David Hamilton
Another of Hamilton's country houses in *mixed modern Gothic* – mullioned and transomed windows, crenellated parapets, tall octagonal castellated finials, and a taller tower. A *porte-cochère* and conservatory are equally Gothic as are the estate **stables**. At the rear of the main house is a small cast-iron **bridge**, *c.*1815-20, of its kind *probably the earliest in Argyllshire*. Hafton House is now a country club, so that much of the wooded estate has been sprinkled with timber-framed chalets of varied design.

Hafton House

ARDNADAM & SANDBANK

Leaving Hafton Estate, the road along the south side of Holy Loch passes the 3-miles-to-Dunoon milestone at **Glen Cottage**, a neat skew-gabled house with bellcast eaves and flying stair, before making a sharp bend at Lazaretto Point. A Baronial **War Memorial**, *c*.1920, signposts the corner.

Sandbank is a one-street working village, its private jetties once given over to the comings-and-goings of a small but world-famous yacht-building industry. Ardnadam, despite its larger more upmarket detached residences, had a working pier, 1858, which at 200ft was *the longest on the upper reaches of the lochs and Firth*.

There is an air of half-hearted short-term husbandry about Sandbank's main street. Only a few properties make it possible to imagine how the village looked in Victorian times: single-storeyed in a slated row at **1-4 Clyde Cottages** or two storeys, cramped at the **Oakbank Hotel** and only slightly more generous in the burnt-out **Argyll Hotel**, *c*.1820.

War Memorial

Above the village of Ardnadam, in a field to the east of Ardnadam Farm, is a prehistoric chamber known variously as *Adam's Cave*, *Adam's Grave* or, simply, *The Cromlech*. The chamber, constructed of slabs of schist, is 10ft 6in. long, entered between two tall standing stones like portal pillars, and covered in part by a massive capstone. It is believed to date from *c*.3700 BC.

There is, too, the ubiquitous tenement, **Oakfield Place**, *c*.1905, a red sandstone wall of canted bays topped off by bargeboarded gablets. But **Benmore View**, 1902, once a reading room, is unique: a roughcast house transformed by vast square dormers in a roof that oversails the walls below to such a distance that its wide-boarded eaves need ogee brackets for support. Uphill to the south, **Sommerville Place**, 1869, reverts to traditional terrace type: three houses, rubble walled, with six gabled dormers and a single attic bay above a bowed corner to the north.

Sandbank Parish Church, 1868

Set by the burn, its gable front has a triple lancet with three trefoil windows below. To the right is a cylindrical belfry tower with a candle-snuffer roof in patterned slate.

Sommerville Place

Sandbank Parish Church

Dumbarton District Libraries

Dick

Few travellers are unaffected by the prospect of the Firth of Clyde. Lord Cockburn, who on several occasions on his *Circuit Journeys* journeyed through Argyll to and from Inveraray, described the experience in his diary on Friday 11 Sept. 1840: *On Monday last, the 7th, we left Strachur for Kilmun, a beautiful day, and a delightful stage of sixteen miles... we had ample time to enjoy the melancholy beauty of Loch Eck, for our steeds did not choose to hasten through the scene... we were in time, after all, for the steamer, which soon swept us out into the busy and glorious Clyde, the most varied, magnificent, and enjoyable of inland seas. The sun was hastening home, and threw his parting light on almost the whole circle of bright and striking towns and villages, by which its edges are specked; on Kilmun, Dunoon, Gourock, Greenock, Helensburgh, and on many hamlets, besides kindling the summits of the finest collection of noble and picturesque mountain peaks in the world.*

KILMUN (*above*)
North of Sandbank a road branches west heading for Colintraive and the Kyles of Bute ferry. **Holy Loch Farm Park** (*left*) sits at the junction spread out in a symmetrical courtyard plan. On the haughlands where the rivers Eachaig and Little Eachaig debouch into the Holy Loch, stands **Courtney's Hotel**, formerly the **Cot House Inn**, a crow-step gabled coaching station, whose origin dates back to 1623. From here the main road north continues up the **Eachaig Valley** and along the shore of **Loch Eck** passing below **Whistlefield Inn** (see p.116), 17th century and later, where the coaching route crossed through Glenfinart to Ardentinny, and on to Strachur, Loch Fyne and Inveraray.

Benmore House, 1862, Charles Wilson, 1874, David Thomson (*below*)
A rambling assemblage of crow-stepped gables, machicolated eaves and bay windows from which a higher more Baronial turreted tower rises, this beautifully landscaped estate mansion now finds itself at the heart of the Younger Botanic Garden. The house once possessed a glass-roofed picture gallery; today, however, it is the richly planted arboretum, gardens and estate walks which attract the visitors.

RCAHMS

Now a recreation centre for Lothian Region, the house has been mutilated by the addition of a crassly designed fire-escape stair. On the other hand, great care has been taken to conserve the courtyard buildings (including clocktower and doocot) of the equally Baronial **steading**, 1874, recently restored, 1989, by PSA architects. Fortunately, too, the estate **lodge**, 1874, and its fine wrought-iron gates are still well preserved.

Close to Courtney's Hotel, the A880 turns back along the northern side of Holy Loch towards Kilmun. **Ardbeg**, *c*.1890, a red and white half-timbered bayed villa, sits cosily in the trees above the road. Half-timbering – this time black and white – is also the idiom of the former **Convalescent Homes**, l873-4, but the three-storey scale and a symmetrical composition of central gables, flanking dormered wings and glazed verandas are inevitably more institutional than domestic.

Top *Ardbeg.*
Above *Convalescent Homes*

Old Kilmun House, from l8th century
In a six bay two-storey-and-basement front, with only slight chamfering of the window jambs relieving the rubble austerity, the pedimented doorpiece is inevitably off-centre. Against one of the crow-stepped gables is a later lower addition, modestly Baronial. A luxuriant garden setting heightens the architectural impact.

Left *Old Kilmun House.*
Below *St Munn's Church*

St Munn's Church, 1841, Thomas Burns
The first church built here was founded towards the end of the sixth century when the Irish saint Mun, a friend of Columba, settled in the sheltered haven of the Loch. Sometime during the l3th century monks from Paisley

Dick

Right *St Munn's Church.*
Below *Campbell Mausoleum*

Dick

Abbey built a new place of worship on somewhat higher ground. In 1442 this Collegiate Church was endowed by Sir Duncan Campbell of Lochawe with a provost and six prebendaries and in 1453 Campbell became the first of many of his clan to be buried here. Of this second building only a roofless tower still stands, looking more like an abandoned keep than the last fragment of a medieval kirk.

The Campbells' *place of interment was within the ancient church; and the access to it continued to be through the body of the parish church till the year 1793 or 1794* when the **Campbell Mausoleum** was erected on the site. Classically organised – a dome on a square – the façade betrays the stylistic ambivalence of its times : pointed Gothic in a crudely Corinthian framework of pilasters and entablature.

Today the Mausoleum is tucked against the rear of the third Kilmun kirk, a plain Gothic T-plan church, 1841, in snecked rubble with a rather slender open-parapeted, pinnacled tower.

The beautiful graveyard has much of interest. A hogback stone may mark the grave of a Pictish king. Many headstones have carving telling the occupation of those whose lives and deaths they record – the oldest, a tailor's stone of 1697. The resting place of Elizabeth Blackwell, *the first woman Doctor in the world*, can be found. On the wall of the ruined tower of the Collegiate Church two coffin covers, employed to deter early 19th century body-snatchers, have been permanently fixed. Most architectural of all is the stone-roofed octagon of the **Douglas Mausoleum**, 1888, burial place of the Indian soldier Gen. Sir John Douglas of Glenfinart (see p.138).

Kilmun had its pier before Dunoon. In 1827-8, the Glasgow marine engineer David Napier bought land on the north shore from the Campbells of Monzie. Nothing but a *paltry clachan* existed prior to Napier's investment but within a few years he had constructed a pier, 1827, built a hotel and six speculative houses, 1829, and had engineered a road cross-country to his estate of Glenshellish at the head of Loch Eck.

Tea Caddies, 1829, David Napier
These six pavilion-roofed rubble houses each
follow a plain three-bay Georgian model and,
though all have been impaired by extraneous
porches, the order of the group is unexpected
and impressive.

Napier's initiatives set a pattern for others to
emulate and Kilmun developed into an
attractive linear village of south-facing villas.
Hillside House, *c.*1840, is plain three-bay
Georgian again, enlivened by an oriental
infection in its porch ironwork. **Glenfinart** is
grander, if stiffly symmetrical, with square
bays and tripartite pilastered dormers. More
typical of later freer formulas, **Ferngrove** is a
mixture of bargeboarded and crow-stepped
gables with an almost rococo profile to its porch
window and a grotto-like garden portal – one of
a number of encrusted entrance archways to be
found along the loch-side.

Above *Tea Caddies*
Left *Younger Hall*

David Napier (1790-1869) was
born in Dumbarton but at the
age of 12 moved to Glasgow.
Fascinated by steam power, he
worked with his father on the
design of a boiler for Henry
Bell's *Comet* and in 1813
established his own works at
Camlachie to manufacture
steam boilers. In 1818 he
collaborated with Denny of
Dumbarton on the first
steamers between Greenock
and Belfast. Further ventures
with shipbuilders in Port
Glasgow and Greenock followed
and Napier's prestige in marine
engineering was assured.

In 1828, having bought
ground on the north shore of
Holy Loch, he began to open up
Cowal. He ran regular steamers
from Broomielaw in the heart of
Glasgow to Kilmun *where
passengers boarded a steam
coach for the short journey to
Loch Eck, where the little
steamship* Aglaia *awaited them.
From the other end of the loch
another steam coach ran to
Strachur, on Loch Fyne, to meet
the boat to Inveraray.*

Village life focused on the churches and village
hall. When the Disruption came, a plain rubble
Free Church, 1843, little more than a gabled
box embedded into the hillside, appeared along
the shore from St Munn's Kirk. The **Younger
Hall**, *c.*1905, is a delightful *mélange* of red
sandstone, roughcast and white paint in which
bargeboarded gable, castellated tower, veranda
and conically roofed corner bow all combine in
Arts & Crafts whimsy.

After a period of depression,
around 1837 he sold off almost
all his Scottish interests and,
for reasons never fully clear,
moved south where he built a
shipyard and engineering
works at Millwall, London. It
was Napier's yard which played
a part in building *Great
Western* and *Great Eastern* for
John Scott Russell and
Isambard Kingdom Brunel.

STRONE & BLAIRMORE
Napier extended his lands east by the purchase
of a three-mile stretch of coastline from Strone
to Blairmore. With the later building of piers
(1847 and 1855), the same seaside development

Above *Cladaigh*.
Right *Craigielee*

Right & below *Creggandarroch,
formerly Oakleigh Villa*

ensued and *a chain of villas and cottages ornés* appeared. **Craigielee** is gabled and bayed with a low pyramid tower. Towers, taller and more Italianate, feature at **Blairmore House**, **Creggandarroch**, formerly Oakleigh Villa, 1863, John Gordon, and **Duart Tower** – the last combining bays, gables, arches and cantilevered Tudor in a fairy-tale concoction above its rocky garden. A recurring element is a two-light canted bay; it appears in several properties on the Blairmore shore and at Cove. One house has a Gothick folly, overgrown and half-hidden in the trees but watched over by what must be the *nonpareil* of garden sculpture – two antlered deer! Most romantic is **Cladaigh**, a rustic cottage villa, busy with timber bays and balconies, looking as if it might have been transported from some Central European forest.

The green rubble Alliance Church has become the **Highgate Hall**, still signposting its religious provenance in a tell-tale vesical window high in the gable. **Strone Church**, 1884, extended 1904, boasts a rather heavy spired belfry rising over a Norman arch porch.

Dick

Dunselma, 1885-6, Rennison & Scott
A high ogee-turreted tower, tied by cable-moulded bonds to the corbels, bays and bartizans below, commands some of the Firth's finest prospects. Dominating the skyline above Strone Point, this extravagant Baronial pile, built as a sailing lodge by the Coats family of Paisley, combines architecture and landscape in wonderful conceit. Down on the Shore Road is **Dunselma Lodge,** trimly responsive to its parent house on the hill.

Left *Dunselma.*
Below *Dunselma Lodge*

Dick

ARDENTINNY

Travel in loch-stabbed Argyll has changed. Two centuries and more ago, routes down into the heartland of Scotland crossed glen and loch by the shortest passage. Today, roads take the long way round and, apart from the few major services on the Firth, the old ferries have all gone. Ardentinny on Loch Long is one of many places deprived of its *raison d'être* by such 'improvements'.

Still little more than a few snug cottages, the village clusters close to its church and inn. The roughcast **church**, 1839, built by the Laird of Glenfinart, has a gabled front with bellcote and porch – neat and tidy, but undistinguished. More attractive is a white-painted stone row, porched and dormered, with a steep half-

Ardentinny Church

Dick

137

Top *Ferry Cottages*.
Above *Ardentinny Hotel*

octagon roof hard by the church door. Across the road by the loch are **Ferry Cottages**, early l9th century, skew-gabled with some rudely cut door pediments.

Ardentinny Hotel, from 18th century
Pressing hard on the road the old plain-faced Scottish house holds centre stage; in the wings, the gabled fronts of later flanking additions. To the rear there is scarcely the same architectural clarity, but more space, trees, lawns, rocks and shingle, and the delightful prospect of the loch.

There has been an inn at Ardentinny for centuries serving the drovers who once ferried their cattle across Loch Long *en route* for Lowland markets. Parts of the present building are said to be almost 400 years old.

Glenfinart House, early l9th century; additions 1895-6
Set back from the shore of Loch Long, at the south end of the road running north by Loch Eck and Glenbranter to Loch Fyne, Glenfinart was raised on the site of an earlier house. It was built by Archibald Douglas in that *mixed English manor-house style* which became so ubiquitous and persistent in Cowal that when extensive enlargements were made in late Victorian times the same architectural idiom was maintained. Rising incongruously in a caravan park, only a forlorn shorn tower remains, lamenting its fate in the motto carved above its porch: *De Tout Mon Coeur*.

Glenfinart House

Dick

INNELLAN
Knockamillie Castle, 16th century

Ravaged in recurrent clashes between Lamonts and Campbells all that remains of this ancient fortalice is a single stand of rubble wall. MacGibbon & Ross detected *a courtyard of considerable size*, but nothing remains to show the extent or architectural character of what was, until the 19th century, almost the only structure of note between Dunoon and Toward.

Notable villas along the shore include: **Glenacre** with a balustraded bay to the left and a gabled square bartizan on the right; **Cluniter**, still more Baronial, with its crowsteps and candle-snuffer stair tower; **Cluniter House**, more true to type but augmented by a neat symmetrical stable block; and, smaller and rougher, **Hoop House**, said to be the oldest inhabited house in the village and built, as might be guessed, by a local cooper. The pattern reaches north to Bullwood where **Rossarden** is particularly trim with its finialled gables and **Woodbine Cottage** has a big segmentally roofed glazed porch added to its symmetrical seaside Gothick. South of the pier **Balnacuil** is similarly quirky, sadly in disrepair, but redeemed by the retention of a fine ironwork porch; **Crossaig Lodge** possesses a good conservatory but makes little of its asset.

Sheltered Housing, 1987-9, SSHA architects
At the junction of Shore Road and Innellan Park, 28 new houses built in polychromatic brick nevertheless succeed in capturing something of the spirit of the place in open timber gables, stringcourses, dormers, etc.

Innellan shoreline

In the 1840s feuing of the coastal strip began and a few years later, a pier, 1850-1, extended 1900, was constructed. Immediately, house building accelerated and a small community, served daily by steamer, first from Greenock and later Wemyss Bay, began to develop – and not just Glasgow's bourgeoisie, for the Coats family from Paisley and the ropemaking Birkmyres of Port Glasgow built here too. Architectural fashions dictated broadly two models for the long line of houses which stretch along the shore north and south from the pier. First, the vaguely Gothic villa, single- or double-gabled in front with peaked dormers, hood mouldings, and perhaps an iron porch; secondly, skew-gabled or piend-roofed, a duller, plainer, Georgian-derived precedent.

Sheltered Housing

Dick

Right *Shore road in times past with Royal Hotel above.* Below *Royal Bar.* Middle *Parish Church.* Bottom *West Church*

John T Rochead (1814-78), the prominent Glasgow architect and designer of some of the city's finest West End terraces, retired briefly around 1870 to Innellan; *apparently his mind had given way under pressure of business and he came to Innellan to recover his health.* The move was a success for Rochead was restored by the peace of the place and *greatly calmed and refreshed in spirit by the quiet worship* which he enjoyed in the Free Church, now the West Church, on Wyndham Road. Fully recovered, he resolved *to express his gratitude to God for his goodness to him by providing the money for the steeple and also for the back gallery to the Church.*

Innellan is redolent with retiral and retreat. A single three-storey tenement and a long terrace of shops and flats give some sense of scale to the pierhead centre of the village but since the closure of the pier in 1972 there is little activity. Uphill, the Baronial **Royal Hotel** has gone, though the red-tiled roof and inventively grouped rubble and ashlar forms of its lodge, now the **Royal Bar**, on Pier Road, are a valuable legacy. So, too, are the village's two remaining churches.

Innellan Parish Church, 1853, enlarged 1866-7
Behind a wide triple-gabled front to Wyndham Road, the church stretches back over the sloping hillside. A massy undercroft buries itself in rhododendrons below transepts and chancel, blunted lancets and ruggedly random rubble intensifying the earth-bound solidity. In the garth hangs the church bell, 1880, cast by C Wilson, Founders, Glasgow.

West Church, 1850, steeple *c*.1870
Built as the Free Church; lanceted Gothic again, though somewhat more aspiring in its proportions. To the south of the five-bay nave is a square tower now bereft of the spire which the architect J T Rochead gifted. Architecturally modest, the church gains distinction from a fine hillside site and the colourful texture of its masonry – grey-green rubble set in red sandstone dressings. Its imaginative conversion into a private house was carried out by architect David Heugh.

TOWARD & LOCH STRIVEN
In 1795, pressure from the people of Rothesay, anxious over the dangers of navigation between Bute and the mainland, failed to persuade the authorities of the need for a lighthouse on Toward Point. Some 17 years passed before

Toward Lighthouse, 1812, was finally built. Its white cylindrical tower, blind lancets in the shaft, rises 63ft to an iron balcony and copper-domed light; below are the chimney-clustered piended roofs of the foghorn machinery buildings looking *rather like a Wee Free kirk*. Like its neighbour on Cloch Point across the Firth, it makes a memorable architectural impact whether seen from land or sea.

Around the light a small community developed: a few houses, a pier, 1863, which failed to attract heavy traffic and closed as early as 1922, and **Toward Church**, c.1840, set on a low-walled platform, a modest three-bay chapel with an arched and spired bellcote above its single gable façade.

Toward Castle, 15th-17th century Stronghold of the Lamonts, the original tower, c.1475, was later extended to the south-east, 1619, with outbuildings gathered around a courtyard to which a splendidly carved round-arched portal with corbelled lugs gave access. In 1646 the castle was besieged by the Campbells who in their attempt to exterminate the Lamont clan, *most barbarously, cruelly and inhumanly murdered several, young and old, yea, sucking children, some of them not one month old*. Following this infamy, the buildings were deserted and fell into ruins.

Top *Toward Lighthouse.*
Above *Toward Castle*

Castle Toward, 1820-1, David Hamilton In 1818 the Glasgow merchant, Kirkman Finlay, bought the lands of Auchavoulin at the south end of the Cowal peninsula, renamed them Toward and began to establish a model estate. Over a period of 20 or so years some five million trees were planted while, not far from the Lamonts' ruined castle, Finlay had a new

Castle Toward

castellated mansion house constructed. Designed by David Hamilton, who considered it one of his best works, Castle Toward is a picturesque asymmetrical spread surmounted by crenellated parapets and *a multiplicity of towers set like the points of a diadem against the purple hills of Argyll.*

Many of these towers date from the 1920s when the house passed into the ownership of Andrew Coats, scion of the thread-making family in Paisley. Coats had the house greatly extended in such similar style and materials that it is difficult to detect the century gap between old and new. Only in the interiors, where the exuberance of some of the plasterwork is almost rococo in spirit, is the later work more apparent.

Knockdow, from *c*.1750
The original house, identifiable as the five-bay quoined front in the centre of the southern façade, antedates the purchase of the estate by the Lamonts *c*.1810, who extended the house with single storey bow-fronted wings. Later, *c*.1830, romantic fashion dictated asymmetrical growth, including a drum stair tower. Next came bow-fronted expansion at first floor, *c*.1870, raising the earlier wings to match the eaves height of the 18th-century core.

Lavish transformations took place between 1921 and 1925, when George Mackie Watson created a symmetrically fronted east wing complete with *porte-cochère*. At the same time he radically altered the internal arrangements to produce a large central room lit by a glazed dome through the drum of which four first-floor balconies, each with charming Ionic column screens, are allowed to intrude. The richly classical interiors of this 1920s conversion were carried out in a variety of exotic hardwoods – mahoganies, sandalwood, almond – from the Lamont estates in Trinidad.

Below *Knockdow.*
Bottom *Inverchaolain Church*

RCAHMS

Dick

Inverchaolain Church, 1912
A simple buttressed church with porch and single transept, it replaced an earlier kirk of 1812. The graveyard contains many 18th-century stones, their inscriptions surprisingly well preserved. It is worth the long single-track drive up the east shore of Loch Striven to come upon this beautiful setting, the church, on a wooded bluff above the loch, surrounded by rhododendrons, gorse and yews.

Rothesay Bay, aquatint by J Clarke, 1824

BUTE

Despite a notorious *liability to severe and sudden rains*, the soft landscape, fertile slopes and sheltered harbours of Bute have attracted settlement from the earliest times. Throughout the island there is evidence of Neolithic and Bronze Age occupation – pottery, axes, querns, cists and cairns as well as standing stones. At least eleven Iron Age strongholds have been identified, none more notable in Scotland than the fortified southern promontory of Dunagoil. Equally distinctive and liberally spread, if less visibly dramatic, are the ruins and relics left by the early Church. From the sixth century Bute must have been an important base from which Christianity spread across western Scotland; chapels dedicated to the many missionary saints of the Celtic Church abound: Ninian, Blane, Macaille, Catan, Colmac, Adamnan, Marnock, Bride.

Viking invasion, however, violently disrupted the Celtic life and culture of the west coast islands and the struggle for power between Norsemen and Scots dragged on for centuries. Rothesay Castle, the island's principal fortress, repeatedly changed hands. In 1230, for example, it was taken by the Norse under Uspak and again, in 1263, by Haakon. That same year, however, after the decisive Battle of Largs fought in the Firth, castle and island were finally secured for the Scottish Crown by Alexander III.

Aerial view, Rothesay

Rothesay Castle: Above *Present day*. Top right *Conjectural restoration, 16th century*. Right *View, 1846*

During the Wars of Independence Rothesay Castle fell to the English, was re-taken by Bruce in 1311, succumbed once more to the English in 1334, only to be recaptured by men loyal to Robert, High Steward of Scotland, the owner of Bute. It became a favoured royal residence of both Robert II and Robert III, who may have died here in 1406. A century later James IV and James V, utilising Rothesay in their subjugation of the Western Isles, made frequent visits and extensively reinforced its defences. It was James IV who, in 1498, made Ninian Stewart hereditary keeper.

In 1544 the Earl of Lennox captured the castle for the English who were again in Rothesay during the Civil War. Cromwell's troops dismantled the structure in 1659 and in 1685 it was burnt out. Years of neglect continued until in the 19th century efforts were made by the hereditary keepers, now Stuarts not Stewarts, to improve the condition of the fabric. During the 1870s, John Patrick Stuart, 3rd Marquess of Bute, undertook major restoration including *the removal of contiguous tenements*. Since then the Butes have maintained a concerned stewardship.

1 **Rothesay Castle**, 13th & 16th century
Set behind its deep moat, once on the sea's edge but now in a picturesque enclave of well-tended lawns, this courtyard castle is unique in Scotland. The commission of Alan, High Steward of Scotland, its circular plan may date from 1204, though opinion differs as to whether the four round towers are original or later 13th-century additions. A forward keep, built in front of the earliest gatehouse, is certainly later – the work, 1512-14, carried out by John and Huchone Cowper, master masons for James IV and James V. Above its vaulted passage leading to the inner yard is a large hall, with a finely moulded fireplace, and what may be the remnant of an oratory.

In the courtyard is the small chapel of St Michael constructed during the 14th-century reign of Robert II. From it a staircase rises to the ramparts. To the east the great wall shows signs of the breach hacked out by the Norsemen in 1230. Some time later the wall must have been heightened since only the lower courses are in ashlar and part of the early parapet can still be seen *sealed up, like a fossil*.

ROTHESAY

Medieval Rothesay received its Royal Charter
from Robert III in 1401, its trading rights
confirmed and extended into free port status by
James VI in 1585. The town clustered around
its ancient fortified stronghold benefiting alike
from Royal preferment, the protection of the
castle and the shelter of a superb anchorage on
the leeward side of the island. Trade must,
however, have been modest and, indeed,
around 1700 Rothesay *fell greatly into decay*, a
fate not perhaps unconnected with the final
sacking of town and castle a generation before
but principally related to the growing
importance of Campbeltown.

By 1760, however, the herring industry had
revived the local economy – to such a
protracted extent that a century later the town
was still putting out more than 500 boats.
Meanwhile, linen and cotton manufacture had
also begun so that by the start of the 19th
century the burgh was growing rapidly. Wood's
Survey, 1825, shows a large harbour, several
mills along the Water of Fad lade, and ribbons
of substantial mansions stretching west and
east around Rothesay Bay. Pigot's *Directory* of
the same year reported that Rothesay had
already become *a fashionable watering place*
and it was this aspect of the town's prosperity
which, despite the collapse of the fishing and
textile industries, assured its future and
continued expansion through the Victorian
period into the 20th century.

Publicising its mild climate
for health and its bay, Rothesay
established itself as the premier
resort on the Clyde for
Glasgow's mercantile gentry
many of whom chose to build on
the island and commute to the
city by steamer and train. By
the 1880s huge numbers of mill
and shipyard workers were
pouring *doon the watter* for
their annual trades week
holiday. So busy was Rothesay
during these summer months
that in a single day as many as
19 different steamers could call
at her piers, many of these
putting in several different
times.

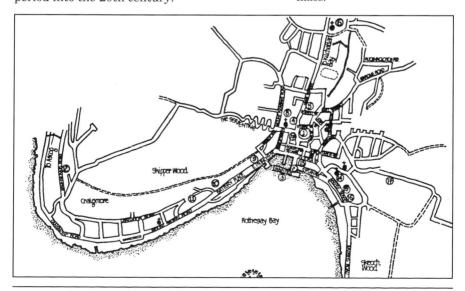

The view across the water from the ferry is still magnificent. Round Bogany Point, Rothesay is revealed, the wide cleavage of the bay dipping between wooded slopes swelling gently on either side. A long necklace of building strung around the edge of the bay heightens nature by artifice: pale olive and cream at the centre along the painted fronts of **Victoria Street** and **Albert Place**, red and grey beyond where tenements and terraces continue the line, and finally ochre in the beaded villas stretching out along the shore to Ardbeg on the west and Craigmore on the east.

View from east

Pier urinals

Rothesay Pier

Building operations began in the mid 18th century. Over a 30-year period from 1752, the **Old Quay** running out from Watergate was constructed. By its completion the boom in the fishing industry was so great that a second pier was needed. This **New Quay**, 1785-90, parallel to the Old on the west, took a 90° turn to create a protected Inner Harbour. With the advent of steam both quays were combined, 1822, and later lengthened, 1899, to give the harbour its present form.

In 1839-40 reclamation extended the shore-line north of Montague Street: Victoria Street and Albert Place could thus be created and in 1869 the Esplanade. Pier Buildings appeared in 1854 and the **Albert Pier** in 1860-5.

Of the turreted Edwardian Pier Buildings (destroyed by fire 1962) only a **cabbies' shelter** and **public toilets** remain. The former is a glazed-cast iron structure in the best tradition of railway architecture, the latter nothing less than astonishing – glazed bricks, mosaic floors, tiled walls, island urinals in black marble vitreous china and glazed cisterns in which patrons could, no doubt, with a flush of pride, watch the miracle of Victorian

3 sanitation. The new **Ferry Terminal**, 1992, a gold-crested, pagoda-roofed pavilion by Strathclyde Region Architects, successfully recaptures some lost nautical zest.

Ferry Terminal

On the made-up ground behind the Inner Harbour the buildings that originally fronted **Guildford Square** have gone. Victims of subsidence, the scar of their removal has yet to heal though recent paving and planting have greatly helped. On the other hand, this greater space beside the pier draws the visitor immediately in to the heart of the old town.

High Street

Bute Estate Offices

The backbone of the town running south from the pier uphill to the High Kirk (see p.149); it passes the Castle with a wall of tenements, which have replaced earlier lower houses, **Castle View** at **45-49**, suitably Baronial for its name and prospect. At **31-43** the castellated parapets and towers of the ancillary offices of the Sheriff Court (see p.150) in Castle Street are equally allusive. Earlier scale returns at **51-53**, *c*.1830, while at the **Bute Estates**

4 **Offices**, 17th century, 1681 on skew, once the Town House of the Butes, a delightful three-storey property projects a crow-step gabled wing to the street. At **61-67**, *c*.1820, a sink remains in the roughcast street wall.

Across the street a seven-stepped **Mercat Cross** replaces the medieval Cross that stood for centuries at the junction with Castle Street. **No 3 Stuart Street**, *c*.1830, a flatted whin-rubble house with dressed surrounds and eaves cornice, incorporates a datestone, 1626-1826, above its entrance. The small symmetrical front of the **Bute Museum**, 1926, has a Palladian window over its pedimented portal. Beyond this the redeveloped backdrop to the Castle has been cruelly mismanaged; narrow old feus combined into wider sites for new buildings whose pronounced horizontality destroys the townscape. The façades of **King Street**'s surviving flats and tenements, now magnificently cleaned, show the lines of what could and should have been done.

1-5 Russell Street

Foley House

High Street has fared better, though its recent housing is perhaps over-agitated in form. Just how powerful a simple but strongly maintained street-line can be is evident in the red tenements at **72-74** High Street and **1-5 Russell Street**, 1902, in a splendid Baronial range with decorative strapwork and barley-sugar downpipes from **14** to **26 Russell Square**, 1877, 1901, and, most of all, at **Mansefield Place** and **Bourtree Place**, the former a polychromatic wall rippling with bays that rise into a mansardic attic, the latter less ebullient but much enhanced by the carvings cut into the bay window corbels. Locked into this late Victorian rigour, **80-86** High Street, *c.*1860(?), older and lower, with some timber bays, preserve an earlier streetwise sense. Incongruous, but nostalgic, too, the former **Ritz Cinema** has only the bruised but monumental self-confidence of a 1930s finned façade to recommend it; it is one of four cinemas that once brought glamour and adventure to the town; the Regal (see p.159) remains too, but the Palace and the De Luxe have gone.

Foley House, late 18th century
Now a hotel, this Georgian two-storey mansion is approached from the High Street through curved screen walls and a tree-lined drive. Its harled façade is orthodoxly pedimented, bounded by pilaster quoins and entered through a narrow pedimented doorway flanked by fluted Ionic pilasters.

As the High Street climbs, it becomes less urban. **Ashtree Cottage**, for example, has the wide eaves and hood mouldings of rural England; **177-179** High Street, *c.*1860, on the other hand, is an uncompromising Scottish tenement. **Rothesay Health Centre**, 1974, Baron Bercott & Associates, is a relaxed grouping of white fascias, glazed porch and monopitch gable. Somewhat stiffer is the just-Gothic front of **Victoria Cottage Hospital**, 1897, J Russell Thomson, its Sheriff Martin Wing, 1927, reiterating the gabled format of the earlier building. On the lawn a glazed timber shelter seems to have strayed uphill from the Esplanade. A little further on is the dried-up niche of **St Mary's Well** set in the old rubble wall below the trees.

High Kirk

6 **High Kirk**, 1796, additions 1906
In 1692, the ruinous parish kirk was replaced by a simple gabled structure orientated north/south and galleried east/west. A century later this was superseded by a higher pavilion-roofed building which followed the established alignment with the two tall arched windows on the south and a pedimented lower storey projecting north. In 1906 further changes, entailing a 90° recasting of the interior and a two-storey pedimented entrance wing lit by pilastered windows, produced the present church.

Close to the south-east corner the ruined walls of the 16th-century chancel survive as **St Mary's Chapel**. A single gable is punctured by a pointed arch window bereft of tracery; within are two tomb recesses containing effigies: an armoured knight under an ogee arch and, opposite, mother and child under a round arch.

The graveyard contains the late 18th-century **Bute Mausoleum**, a weatherbeaten sandstone gabled cell. Rudely eclectic, it combines baroque broken pediments, Gothick tracery and six squat neoclassical obelisk finials.

Above *Bute Mausoleum.*
Left *St Mary's Chapel*

Below *9 Castle Street*.
Middle *Sheriff Court*.
Bottom *Trinity Church*

Walker

RCAHMS

Walker

TOWN CENTRE: East
On the east side of Guildford Square, **1-21
Albert Place**, the regal reflection of Victoria
Street, preserves nobility of scale and detail –
consoles, dentilled eaves, and, at the **Royal
Hotel**, a columned and pilastered porch.

A curved corner leads into **Bishop Street**.
1-9, *c.*1780, built through the orchard of the
medieval Bishop's House, incorporates a lithic
relic with the motto *Pax Intrantibus, Salus
Exeuntibus* (Peace to those entering, Health to
those leaving). Only half the inscription is
original, inserted here after being found
nearby. From **19** to **27**, *c.*1780, single-storey
cottages step up the street maintaining heavy
eaves mouldings. **16-20**, *c.*1830, with in-and-out
quoining, is two-storey and preserves an early
shopfront at **No 16**. Varying this older character
are some tenements and a rather grand **post
office**, 1896, which, somewhat Netherlandish
in its classical format, raises a pedimented
scrolled gable from a balustraded parapet.

Bishop Street turns into **Castle Street** and
at once there is a sense of being at the civic
heart of the town's affairs. This has much to do
with the breadth, containment and dip of the
street but more perhaps with the architecture.
8-24 keep common eaves along most of the
south side of the street; **22** has tripartite
windows on each side of a Roman Doric door, a
pattern repeated across the street at **9** where
an Ionic portico and large pedimented dormer
lend added sophistication to the offices of **Bute
Housing Association**.

7 **Sheriff Court**, 1832, James Dempster;
enlarged 1865
In 1831 Parliamentary authority was given to
building *a gaol, court house, and offices for the
burgh and the county*. The result was a square-
cut fort, built in a dark olive stone with lighter
sandstone dressings, towered and battlemented
but decidedly dour. Not even tall triple lancet
windows seem able to lighten its grim solidity.

8 **Trinity Church**, 1843-5, Archibald Simpson
A Disruption Free Kirk, it sets great store by
its angle-buttressed tower facade. *The ogee,
double-curvature opening in the spire, the ogee
moulding round the tower, and the leafy
concrescences that crown the corner pinnacles of
the tower parpaet bespeak the influence of the
Decorated*, but only just, for otherwise the
church is relentlessly restrained.

Castle Buildings

A spectacular pile-up of flatted housing advancing and recessing through three and four storeys from the east end of Castle Street: a magnificent architectural accompaniment to the start of The Serpentine.

A walk along Castle Street and up **Serpentine Road** by Castle Buildings is a memorable experience. There is pleasure in the townscape in the ascent and in the views to be had looking back down on town and bay. After a short climb **Bishop's Terrace** cuts off to the left, a one-sided street not without minor architectural incident: **1-2** is pedimented but semi-detached with concave ingoes to its coupled entrances; **3** has a double forestair, **5** a gabled doorpiece; **9** an octagonal bow of cast-iron mullions added to an earlier symmetrically winged house of c.1840; and at the end is **Beechwood**, a substantial Victorian villa, below which a path leads off through **Skipper Wood**. To the right is **Mount Pleasant Road** with two stretches of rough whin tenements – **Windsor Place**, c.1895, with red sandstone dressings; **Osborne Place**, 1897, with ochre – and at **30-34**, a fine painted terrace, its pilastered quoins and doorways linked through in a good eaves cornice.

3 Bishop's Terrace

CRAIGMORE & ASCOG

The eastern side of the Bay starts at **East Princes Street** in high urban style. **Albert Mansions**, in which the **Golf Bar** with its Glasgow Style bar gantry is not to be missed, is a red ashlar tenement, canted bays rising from shop fascias, cornices crossing at each floor level. Next comes **Victoria Mansions** – but it is scarcely a fitting marriage. The street continues, however, at tenement scale in 9 **Duncan's Halls**, **21-23**, 1879, a palatial piece

Duncan's Halls

of French *beaux-arts* theatricality. At **27**, **Lady Mary Mansions**, *c*.1905 (?), reaches five walk-up floors of bay-windowed flats, as does **33**, **Bute Mansions**, 1906. But at **37-42**, *c*.1840, an earlier terrace scale begins: built in local greenstone, **37** and **38** are best, with doorpieces of fluted pilasters; **41** worst, by misguided virtue of massive dormers and a widened window at first floor. **43-44**, 1843, banded in droved sandstone, is elegantly plain.

Battery Place, taking its name from the defences raised here when Napoleon threatened invasion, is at first plain two- and three-storey gable-to-gable. **No 7**, formerly the Prince of Wales Hotel, is a three-tiered chest with the drawers pulled out from top to bottom. At **17-17a**, 1914, a majestic red tenement rears up. **Glendale** is special: much glass and a five-light bow with cast-iron mullions reducing in the attic beneath a concave turreted roof crested in a coronet of iron.

Detached houses now predominate. **Battery Lodge**, 1827, much altered in 1910, asymmetrically Arts & Crafts, is half-timbered and balconied with some turn-of-the-century leaded glass. Finally, at the corner of Glenburn Road, a wide flight of steps leads up to the 10 pedimented porch of the **public baths**, 1875-6. Designed by J R Thomson as the Royal Aquarium, there is something of a princely folly feel about this neat little *palais*.

Top *Battery Place*. Above *Glendale*. Right *Public baths, formerly the Royal Aquarium*

11 **Glenburn Hotel**, 1843, John M Crawford; rebuilt 1892-4
Wide lawns step back steeply from the shore up to this high hydropathic on the hill. No modest *palais* this; lower wings project left and right of a towered centre while an arched loggia with extensions in light ironwork unifies the

spreading façade. The approach from below inspires more awe than welcome – though perhaps yachtsmen, climbing up from their mooring, are less intimidated.

Glenfaulds, *c.*1880
Last and most daring of the tenements; all four storeys, articulated in a wide canted bay flanked by end bows, seem little more than glass. Detailing is vigorous: consoled eaves, cast-iron mullions, fine storm doors.

Above *Glenfaulds*. Left *19-27 Mount Stuart Road*

From **19** to **27 Mount Stuart Road** the first of Craigmore's sea-front terraces stretches out between its coupled end gables. Intervening, **Craigmore St Brendan's Church**, 1888-9, David A Crombie, retains the pinnacled Perpendicular Gothic belfry from the old church, though the new shallow pitched nave gable behind looks second-best. Then comes **Elysium Terrace**, 1875, a symmetrical group of five mansions in a convincing Alexander Thomson manner, **Royal Terrace**, 1877, and, opposite Craigmore Pier, 1877, the three semi-detached houses of **Albany Terrace**, 1882, all the same designer varying the mixture of thin pilaster mullions, decorative bargeboards and ironwork porches: inventive and urbane.

Royal Terrace

153

As early as 1786 sea bathing was one of the advertised attractions of Rothesay. In 1840 it was the *remarkably mild and genial* air which made the town *the Montpellier of Scotland*. Following the fashion of these times, Rothesay advertised itself as a spa, adding the attraction of mineral springs to its other claims to be the premier resort on the Clyde. Not far beyond Craigmore Pier *a net pavilion* – a light tent-like structure of lacy cast-iron – was erected over the spring and the water sold to daring holiday-makers at a penny a glass.

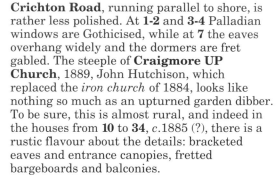

Crichton Road, running parallel to shore, is rather less polished. At **1-2** and **3-4** Palladian windows are Gothicised, while at **7** the eaves overhang widely and the dormers are fret gabled. The steeple of **Craigmore UP Church**, 1889, John Hutchison, which replaced the *iron church* of 1884, looks like nothing so much as an upturned garden dibber. To be sure, this is almost rural, and indeed in the houses from **10** to **34**, *c.*1885 (?), there is a rustic flavour about the details: bracketed eaves and entrance canopies, fretted bargeboards and balconies.

12 **Tor House**, 1855, Alexander Thomson
Set above the bay at High Craigmore this was perhaps something of a trial run for *ideas which flowered so magnificently in the Double Villa* which Thomson built at Langside, Glasgow, a year later; there are the same shallow-pitched roofs, the pilaster-mullioned bay and the block porch set in the internal angle of the plan. But there is also the belvedere first used upriver at Craig Ailey, Kilcreggan (see p.111). Indeed Thomson's eclecticism is well represented: Egyptian chimneys, Greek interior decoration, Italianate tower.

Top *Tor House*. Above *Sewage screening chamber*

Round **Bogany Point**, past the battlemented concrete dome of a shoreside **sewage screening chamber**, the residential ribbon continues. **Mount Carmel Convalescent Home** is a muscular villa with canted bays, a columned porch and a *cracker motif* balustrade at the eaves. **Madras House** has a balconied veranda and some fine ironwork. **Craigend** is almost Regency with arched sashes and an even more splendid veranda. **Montford**

House, *c*.1850, is plain and symmetrical with
another excellent iron balcony, while at
Millburn it is decorated bargeboards which
attract the eye. Much grander is **Ascogbank**,
c.1840, with its Greek Doric porch and an
ashlar façade articulated by coupled Ionic
pilasters. Higher up is **Ardencraig**, *c*.1860, *a
large and exceedingly handsome mansion, built
after a plan modernised from the French* by
George Miller, a Liverpool merchant.

Ascog Church, 1843, David Hamilton
Already built when the Disruption occurred, it
became one of the first Free Churches. A
shallow-pitched gable-end façade, dignified by
a blind Palladian window over a projecting
porch, presents itself to the road. At the sea
end is a square Italianate belfry rising in three
recessing stages.
   On the shore to the north are the ruined
walls of an abandoned 18th-century **salt kiln**
looking more like some defensive peel than any
manufactory.

Ascog Church

Ascog House
Through four carved gate posts which belie an
overgrown and ever-diminishing drive lies this
rather ungainly Victorian Baronial
enlargement of an older building dating from
1678. Its near neighbour, **Ascog Lodge**,
c.1820, is more attractively abstemious:
standard three-bay Georgian with a blinded
tripartite over the door. In a thickly romantic
garden is **Ascog Hall**, 1843, a fairy-tale cluster
of witch-hatted towers and turrets.

TOWN CENTRE: West
Looking out on Rothesay Bay **Victoria Street**
is unified by scale and by colour too, for almost
the entire wall of building west to Coall
Gallowgate has been painted a pleasant cream
with pale olive highlighting the stone dressings.
At **13-15** there are two Thomsonesque
doorways; **21-25** is strongly symmetrical with
tripartite windows surmounted by a coupled
chimney arch; and matching curved corners at
37 and **39** flank the entrance into **Tower
Street**. The steep roofs of the **Victoria Hotel**,
lacily crowned with ironwork, are richly French
in character. Only the low nave gable of
St Paul's Episcopal Church, breaks the
continuity, marking the corner with Deanwood
Place in a small belfry pinnacle.

Victoria Hotel

Winter Garden

RCAHMS

When Queen Victoria sailed into Rothesay Bay in August 1847 she referred in her diary to a *pretty little town, built round a fine bay, with hills in the distance, and a fine harbour. The people cheered the Duke of Rothesay* [the title bestowed on the heir apparent to the throne since 1398] *very much, and also called for a cheer for the 'Princess of Great Britain'. When we went on deck after dinner, we found the whole town brilliantly illuminated, with every window lit up, which had a very pretty effect.*

13 **Winter Garden**, 1923-4, John Stephen
On pierhead or promenade, the lightweight light-filled architecture of glass and steel always seems to conjure up that *frivolity and sense of gaiety wholly appropriate to a seaside resort*. Here, in the esplanade gardens, this fairy-tale palace of varieties built by the burgh's surveyor, using the engineering skills of MacFarlane's Saracen Foundries, is no exception. Pagoda-roofed towers flank the entrance to a domed hall over which tapering steel beams arc up gently like the spokes of a giant umbrella. Out of the rain and into a dream, the Fair Fortnight holidaymakers would test the mettle of Glasgow's comedians. After a decade of neglect, the Winter Garden has been saved for a new generation's enjoyment.

From the shore front **Gallowgate** curves back into town in a two-storey bow. Across the street the **post office** still has its Victorian shopfront in which a consoled broken pediment quaintly stresses the street end. Gallowgate predates the buildings on the reclaimed land of Victoria Street, its flats and shops lower and rougher but more characteristic of the older town. A heavily quoined corner at **Bridge Street** bears the date 1780.

In **Montague Street**, all architectural aspects of Rothesay's townscape are thrown together. **Nos 45-49** present the oldest two-storey scale in a series of gable-to-gable properties (note the squinched dormers at **57-59** which somehow manage to keep a common eaves line). The **TSB Building**, 1979, Roxby, Park & Baird, tries to re-establish this streetscape in neo-vernacular: materials and forms are

imaginatively deployed though the detailing is
sometimes just too clever. There is, however,
no consistent model – higher tenements crop
up irregularly; symmetrical corners into
Tower Street survive; at **85**, art deco in the
red sandstone fin and chevron motifs of
Woolworths; and at **Presto** crass, brash
Modernism – yet it scarcely matters for the
streetline is well defined and full of activity.

In **Bridgend Street** the red sandstone front of
Bridgend Church, 1908, now **St Andrew's
Church Hall**, has a stimulating turn-of-the-
century infusion – in the leaded glass, in an
oddly offset belfry and in an astonishing roof
ventilator.

Bridgend Church

Bridge Street, which extended Montague
Street west after the bridging of the Water of
Fad stream in 1768, is all – or almost all –
flats: **14**, *c.*1850, is symmetrical in plain
painted ashlar with a scroll-based façade
chimney; **20-22**, *c.*1850, rubble-built, preserves
its 16-pane sash windows on the upper floors.
But **24-28**, *c.*1840, are lower in Aberdeen bond
masonry, though **28** has been raised into a
second floor. **Auburn Cottage**, *c.*1820, is lower
still, a rubble cottage with a moulded eaves
course. At the head of the street high on the
side of **Chapel Hill** is **Ivybank**, *c.*1820, a
pavilion-roofed mansion, late Georgian in type
but romanticised by Gothick glazing bars.

Along the banks of the Water of Fad lies that
part of the town which saw the early growth of
the textile industry. In 1778-89 an old flax mill
was fitted up, by Englishmen, with the first
cotton-spinning machinery installed in
Scotland. More mills followed and housing for
the workers, who frequently carried on
spinning and weaving in their own homes too,
was built. Along **Mill Street** and **John Street**,
1805, some of the earliest of these cottages still
survive, those in John Street built by the
Cotton Mill Society having been pleasantly
restored. An admirable local policy of
rehabilitation has also saved the flats at **17-21
Russell Street** complete with their outside
stairs, and round the corner at **2 Union
Street**, the rude classical charm of **Colbeck
Place** has been revealed, rubble-built but
distinguished by a wide doorpiece with
Doric entablature and fluted pilasters. In

Rothesay claims to be the site
of *the first cotton mill
established in Scotland*. Thanks
to the enterprise of Englishmen
familiar with the new spinning
machinery invented by
Arkwright – protected by
patent in England but not in
Scotland – a mechanised
installation was set up in an old
flax mill in the town in 1779.
By the second half of the 19th
century the industry had
declined and in 1882 the last
mill finally closed down. At the
end of the Second World War,
however, thanks to the
initiative of Lord Bute, whose
family had first helped attract
the industry to the island,
weaving was revived. Since
1966 the production of fashion
and furniture fabrics has once
more been put on a successful
commercial footing.

Colbeck Place

Above *30 Columshill Street.*
Right *Bute Fabrics*

Columshill Street more millworkers' housing
has been given a fresh lease of life – note,
particularly, **30** Columsmill Street, *c.*1845 (?),
which may well be the smallest flatted house in
Scotland – though here an otherwise
residential townscape is cruelly dominated by
the red Byzantine bulk of **St Andrew's
Church**, 1923, Reginald Fairlie.

**During the Napoleonic
Wars**, as the steam engines in
Rothesay's mills became
increasingly expensive to
operate owing to the cost of
imported coal, the mill-owners
in the town were threatened
with bankruptcy. Convinced
that water power could still
save the day, the engineer
Robert Thom (1775-1847),
himself a mill-owner, began
building dams, aqueducts, cuts
and sluices, *c.*1820, from Loch
Fad to the mill lade, draining
the marshes and greatly
increasingly hydraulic
efficiency.

These cuts can still be seen,
e.g. at the Lovers' Walk by the
Meadows, while there are also
several small stone bridges
built to allow cattle and carts to
cross the stream, e.g. in the
Scalpsie/Quien area.

Thom, who was also
responsible for an even larger
system of water cuts at Loch
Thom, Greenock, died at his
home at Ascog estate. He is
buried in Rothesay kirkyard.

Bute Fabrics
Rothesay's textile tradition is perpetuated in a
long white-harled building which, on its eastern
side, is thoroughly mill-like but on the west has
17 bays of repetitive sash windows, pedimented
at the centre, that might almost betray its
orphanage origins. Yet there is nothing
institutional here, rather a sense of almost
residential intimacy which the trees and gardens
to Barone Road do much to sustain.

Barone Road begins the climb out of town
to cross the island from east to west. What look
like suburban villas are flatted houses with
rear access stairs; traditional Scottish life-style
in up-market camouflage. But detached
dwellings increasingly appear, each with
qualities to remark: **25- 27** with gabled
pilastered doorways; **37**, **39** and **41** sharing a
penchant for groups of arched windows. Even
the marvellously inventive buildings of
Auchnacoloich Road, *c.*1903, bustling with
gables, bays and balconies (and some turn-of-
the-century glasswork) are not the Arts &
Crafts mansions they appear to be but a series
of four-in-block flats and semi-detached villas.

WEST END

The western side of Rothesay Bay is defined first by **Argyle Street** curving gently in parallel with the Esplanade. There is some painted continuity with Victoria Street but sandstone, ochre and red, predominates. The scale is higher: **7-10**, 1882, four-storey ashlar with elaborate mouldings; **17-20**, 1902, and **27**, also four, clean-cut tenements with bays, the latter with some fine skyline ironwork. Set back from the street the symmetrical Romanesque-detailed front of the **West Church**. 1846, Charles Wilson, still preserves height in its slender pinnacled spire despite its retiring location. The **Regal Cinema**, 1937, Alec Cattanach, pushes forward aggressively, brickbanded wings framing a finned faience front.

16 **Rothesay Pavilion**, 1937-8, James Carrick The set piece of the front. International Style Modernism at its best with little if anything of its period to equal it in Scotland. A fully glazed bowed wing cantilevers to the left with another cantilevered canopy over the second-floor terrace above. Suave, stylish and *soigné*.

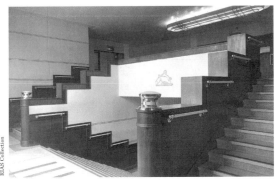

Top *West Church*. Above *Regal Cinema*. Left *Rothesay Pavilion, staircase*. Below *Rothesay Pavilion*

The painter **George Leslie Hunter** (1879-1931) was born in Rothesay. At the age of 13, however, he emigrated to San Francisco where he later found work as an illustrator. Before he could hold his first one-man show his paintings were lost in the earthquake of 1906. Back in Glasgow he continued to paint, on several occasions visiting France where he was strongly influenced by Cézanne. Hunter, and his contemporaries, Cadell and Peploe, together with J D Fergusson, became known as the Scottish Colourists, their paintings introducing a Post-Impressionist freshness into the Scottish art scene. In Hunter's work his Loch Lomond paintings are outstanding; *as fine as any Matisse*, said Peploe.

On **Chapelhill Road**, the **Old Manse** and **2-4 York Terrace** have light Regency-like balconies. Seeming to break free from the cliff face, the tower spire of **Rothesay Free Church**, 1860, rises above an equivocating double-doored porch. **Academy Terrace**, below but still looking over Argyle Street, is a black-and-white composition of half-timbered gables. Above Academy Road on the hilltop site of the ancient chapel of St Bride, demolished 1860, is the former **Museum**, 1873, of the Archaeological & Physical Society, castellated Gothic with a battlemented tower enjoying one of the island's most panoramic views.

17 **Rothesay Academy**, 1956-9, Harvey & Scott
The jutting grid of the main classroom block was said to have *a strange quality of arrested movement ... something of the braced economy of a ship about to be launched.* A generation later this ambivalent description seems still valid; but whether such bulk, frozen on the hill, is fair exchange for J R Thomson's Gothic Revival school, 1869, is doubtful. An arched window built into the wall is all that recalls the original building.

At the corner of McKinlay Street and Argyle Terrace sits a plain but well set pavilion-roofed Georgian house, *c.*1820, semi-detached with Roman Doric doors. **Argyle Terrace**, *c.*1820, is a delightful street of attic dormered cottages, some with forestairs. **Argyle Place** continues north round the bay towards Ardbeg, houses mostly two-storey with dormers, **11** having an attractive Ionic doorway and **6-7** being something of an exception in Rothesay with bargeboarded gable, consoled bay and faceted conical roof. Even here on the edge of town a high tenement appears, **Argyle Mansions**, with full height bays and regular sill-level string-mouldings.

ARDBEG
Going north out of Rothesay towards Ardbeg, the edge of **Skeoch Wood** marches with the promenade. Across the road the **bathing station** guards the shore like a stepped pillbox emplacement, stairs leading down below its corona-lit concrete dome to a ruined sun terrace. Like Craigmore and Ascog, Ardbeg is essentially post-1870 *room with a view* overspill from Rothesay. But here, the atmosphere is more village than suburb: flatted terraces, some shops, a bowling green and a few older relics tucked out

Lovely Cottage

Walker

of sight behind the street-front housing. Only the red-tiled roof and chunky timber porch of the boldly named **Lovely Cottage**, 1879, on **Gortans Road**, possesses an out-of-the-ordinary romantic quirkiness.

The houses on **Ardbeg Road** enjoy a view over the bay which their modest architectural quality scarcely merits. **Woodside**, awkwardly raised from two to three storeys, has the cast-iron mullions which repeatedly recur along Rothesay's sea front; **Tigh-Na-Mara** sits back from the road, bargeboarded and hood-moulded; but a tenement at **Toward View**, 1910, vertically stressed with twin chimney shafts, reasserts the street edge; **Gravel Bank**, skew-gabled with a good doorpiece, is plain but dignified. In the midst of all this is the wheel-windowed gable of **Ardbeg Baptist Church**, 1855, shouldered by dormers over the gallery stairs.

Past the **Thomson Fountain**, 1867, the coast road continues as Marine Place and then as **Shore Road**. **Millerston House**, and **Aros-Na-Mara**, for example, are both enriched by delicate ironwork porches. **The Cottage** is older and simpler, a neat skew-gabled dwelling with eaves cornice and pilastered doorpiece. Rather similar, but grander by virtue of its two storeys and piended single-storey wings, is **4 Shore Road**.

Aros Na-Mara

Walker

North Bute Parish Church, 1886,
William McGibbon
Originally St Ninian's, the church is now the place of worship for the displaced congregations of St Bruoc's and St Colmac's. There is an Early Decorated feel with a plate-traceried window in the nave gable but the square tower, crested in finials and stepping parapets, has a dramatic Romanesque solidity.

Port Bannatyne

PORT BANNATYNE

Since the word Kames is derived from *camus* meaning *bay*, the description Kames Bay is something of a tautology. Kamesburgh, however, makes more sense, though the later Port Bannatyne name does indicate the long familial association of the Bannatynes which lasted from the 13th century until 1780 when the line died out.

Kames Castle, 16th century
The Bannatynes' castle at Kames Bay, a squat harled tower house with a high battlemented parapet, behind which rises a crow-step gabled caphouse, may date from the 14th century, although MacGibbon and Ross prefer a later 16th century ascription. The upper work (possibly by David Bryce) is certainly of more recent date, as are the Baronialised steadings clustered around.

Kames Castle drawn by Robert Carrick c.1850

The Bannatynes of Kames can be traced back as far as the time of Alexander III ... chamberlains to the Stewart kings when Bute formed part of the royal property.
MacGibbon & Ross, Volume 3

Situated on the south side of Kames Bay, Port Bannatyne – Kamesburgh as it was known until its acquisition by the Marquess of Bute in the 1860s – is small but compact, a planned community of two parallel streets following the flattened V configuration of the shoreline. At the centre is the **Old Quay**, 1801, repaired 1962. In general, scale and quality are mixed, though the extra height of later hotel and tenement accommodation, built in the turn-of-the-century holiday boom years when

Caledonian steamers called regularly at the Pier, 1857, and trams brought the trippers round from Rothesay, is at least offset by the wide esplanade.

On **Castle Street** there is no such openness to compensate. At the west end, city-scale tenements end at **Angus Place**, 1895. At the east end is an urban chasm: on one side **Buckingham Terrace**, an ashlar tenement with canted bays; on the other, at **1-19**, four close-packed flatted blocks of comparable bulk each reached by steps climbing up from the pavement. In the middle, however, are rehabilitated two-storey terraces, white-painted, plain and neat, the dormers and door at the rear of **29-38** given a jaunty new nautical look, 1986, by John Wilson Associates.

Wester Kames Tower, reconstructed 1897-1900, Robert Weir Schultz
When Schultz was commissioned by the 3rd Marquess of Bute to rebuild Wester Kames he found an unexceptional ruin, c.1700, standing scarcely more than 12ft high. From this he created a thoroughly convincing Baronial conjunction of four-storey gabled tower, five-storey gable-capped cylinder, and corbelled stair turret. The stone dressings are finely detailed with roll mould rybats, while a thin brick line subtly and respectfully marks the extent of the original ruin.

Top *Castle Street.*
Middle *Buckingham Terrace.*
Above *29-38 Castle Street.*
Left *Wester Kames Tower*

The Stewarts have been lairds on Bute since the 14th century when Robert II granted land and the hereditary Sheriffdom of Bute to his natural son, John, The *Black Stewart*. In 1498, on the authority of James IV, the family were made hereditary keepers of Rothesay Castle and lived there until the castle's destruction in 1685. Thereafter they occupied the Mansion House in the High Street. In 1703 Queen Anne created the Bute earldom and in 1718 the building of Mount Stuart was begun by James, the 2nd Earl.

During the 18th century the power and prestige of the Butes increased, the 3rd Earl advancing his career from tutor to George III to Minister of the Crown and finally Prime Minister. Benefiting from such eminence his son John, the 4th Earl, became Baron Cardiff in 1776 and 20 years later was created 1st Marquess of Bute.

With titles went land and wealth, not only on Bute itself where by 1840 the family owned all but one-seventh of the island but particularly in South Wales where the development of mining and docks had produced an immense fortune. And with wealth went patronage, no Maecenas more munificent than John Patrick, the 3rd Marquess. Influenced by the Oxford Movement in his youth, he converted to Catholicism in 1868, his building projects testifying to both family prosperity and piety. In Wales he engaged William Burges on the design of Cardiff Castle, 1868-81, and Castell Coch, 1875-81; on Bute he not only created a new Mount Stuart complete with its vast chapel, but began the repair of Rothesay Castle, rebuilt Wester Kames and preserved the ancient cell of St Blane's; while elsewhere in Scotland he instigated restoration work at Falkland Palace and Pluscarden Priory.

A similar if less expansive addiction to heritage and conservation continues to ennoble the family's stewardship, most notably marked by the present Lord Bute's Presidency of the National Trust for Scotland but evident too in the careful design control of the island's farm buildings exercised by Bute Estates.

RCAHMS

BUTE : North

Half-way across the island to Ettrick Bay, **St Colmac's Parish Church** (*above*), 1836, with its dumpy belfry tower inset in the east gable, sits roofless and abandoned in a walled graveyard more cared for than the kirk itself. There is an ancient Celtic cross engraved on a standing stone in a field near East St Colmac's Farm. In the extreme north-west of the island, at Kilmichael, fragments of the ruined walls of **St Macaille's Chapel** stand on a grassy knoll protecting a stone slab altar – a remote forgotten fane by the shores of the Kyles of Bute.

BUTE : South

The road west from Rothesay leads to the once thriving fishing village of **Straad**, a quiet place now with neither harbour nor fishing boats. On St Ninian's Point are the remains of **St Ninian's Chapel**, sixth or early seventh century; an altar found here with a relic holder cavity is the only one of its kind in Scotland. Across the bay, just off the road south to Scalpsie Bay, are the meagre remains of **Kilmory Castle**.

Stewart Hall, 1760

A delightful harled house of rugged but civilised Scottish classicism, its principal characteristic is the heavy rustication of quoins, jambs and keystones. The principal façade, to the south, has a projecting pedimented centre capped by urns and stressed not by a porch but by a vigorous Palladian motif with strongly fluted columns. Lower wings project; that to the west extended, 1975, in deferential detail and stunningly accented by a 10-sided conservatory pavilion.

Woodend House, 1824

When Edmund Kean chose this site at the Butt of Woodend for his sanctuary at Bute he found it *the most beautiful place in the world*. A narrow track penetrates deep into the wooded western slopes of Loch Fad, passes through the lodge gateposts he had built (the four piers carry busts of Massinger, Shakespeare, Garrick and Kean himself), continues in leafy mystery until with unexpected casualness it comes upon the house; across a sloping lawn, hemmed in by the wood, is the framed prospect of the loch.

Often referred to as Kean's Cottage, the great actor's hideaway house is a proud little Georgian mansion, holding itself erect in high 24-pane sash windows. There is a columned porch, the walls are roughcast with plain surrounds, the roof is piended and short single storey wings recess behind the façade.

Above *Edmund Kean gate pier, Woodend House*. Left *Woodend House*

For Edmund Kean, the *celebrated tragedian*, Woodend was indeed a sanctuary. His affair with Mrs Cox and the trial which followed – in which he was successfully sued by Mrs Cox's husband – had tarnished his public image; he drank heavily, bouts of depression were frequent. Not surprisingly, his wife, Mary, was less than enthusiastic about being buried in Bute, recalling in a letter how *he took 22 acres of land from Lord Bute's factor – Lord Bute's property – as sterile – as damp as foreign – as desolate as you can conceive – built and furnished a House in a spot where there was no road or any creature within three miles of the place ... it was a madness done by the desire of Mrs Cox to hide me in and ended in utter ruin to us.*

Kerrycroy, from 1803

In 1703, the 1st Earl of Bute procured a charter turning his entire estate into a burgh of regality. A century later, the 1st Marquess recast the tiny community clustered at his gates. At first only four single-storey U-plan cottages and an inn – *windows after the Gothic style* – were symmetrically set in the arc of this attractive bay, while a reconstruction of the old quay, from which a daily post-boat ferry connected Bute to the mainland at Largs, was undertaken using large coursed blocks of stone laid to a gently curved plan extending the soft sweep of the shore. Two Tudor Revival semi-detached villas were inserted in the late 19th century. Respectful of the earlier layout, neither they nor the village green (complete with maypole) which they face are in any sense Scottish.

Kerrycroy

RCAHMS

Mount Stuart

Mount Stuart, 1718-22; rebuilt from 1879
Past the Gothicised **North Lodge**, early 19th
century, the estate driveway begins. The
planting, begun in 1718, was munificent, the
architecture splendid. The first mansion, 1718-
22, was the work of Alexander McGill
commissioned by the 2nd Earl to create
something grander than the family's Mansion
House (see p.147) on Rothesay High Street.
McGill responded with a wide-fronted
pedimented house of three storeys flanked by
lower pavilions all in *a simple dignified style of
country-house architecture probably derived
largely from Sir William Bruce*, architect of
Kinross House and Hopetoun. The central
block of the house was rebuilt, *c.*1740, to
William Adam's design, keeping McGill's side
pavilions. In 1769 James Craig, creator of
Edinburgh's First New Town, completed a five-
week survey at Mount Stuart no doubt with a
view to further additions or alterations, but it
is not clear whether proposals were ever
prepared or implemented.
  In 1877 a fire which destroyed the family
home was less catastrophe than opportunity:

Robert Rowand Anderson was engaged and, over the next decade, a new Mount Stuart took shape. The marble-halled plan, *a large cube containing a smaller cube inside*, was simple. On the other hand, in keeping with the 3rd Marquess's espousal of Roman Catholicism, Anderson's vast square mansion indulges in an orgy of ecclesiastical medievalising. To the north a huge **Chapel**, 1897-1902, also by Anderson, even replicates the tower of Zaragoza Cathedral. It is all perhaps too much. Only the house's third-floor eaves gallery – an afterthought – and its splendidly dormered roof keep a suitably secular lid on eclectic excess. While all this was going on, the Marquess's other most favoured architect William Burges was at work for him in Wales building Cardiff Castle, 1868-81, and Castell Coch, 1876-81. Burges's only contribution to Mount Stuart is a small **oratory**, 1873-5, in one of the McGill wings which survived the fire. But it was his team of craftsmen, carvers and painters who enriched the interiors of Anderson's great pile.

The estate's **Home Farm**, two storeys with rolled skews, dates from 1777. Close to the sea-shore, not far from Kerrycroy, is a T-plan **church**, early 18th century, with bellcoted gables and Gothick windows probably the work of McGill; it serves with dignified ecumenical indifference as a family mausoleum.

At the extreme southern end of the island some of Bute's most memorable sites are to be found. On the western seaward side is the dramatic vitrified fort of **Dunagoil**; rich in archaeological pickings it has yielded more than any other such site in Scotland about its Iron Age inhabitants' style of living: moulds for spears, spinning whorls, bodkins, needles, rings, beads and bracelets.

Garrochty, 1898-1901
A gabled villa with ancillary aspirations to gentlemanly farming. Built by Sir William McEwan, a crusty but brilliant surgeon who, among many firsts, instituted the modern regime of nurses' training. A ten-minute walk uphill from the road-end at Garrochty leads to the remains of a secluded settlement, less ancient but still old, strangely moving, and beautiful St Blane's Church.

Garrochty

Walker

St Blane's Church from the air

St Blane's Church, 12th century
Up over a grassy crest in a hidden hollow, the
ruins of St Blane's Church sit on a raised
graveyard. An outer garth marks the extent of
the monastic community founded by St Catan
in the sixth century. On the west is a protective
cliff at the base of which is a **well** and the
remains of several cells. A circular structure
built with large boulders, the **Devil's
Cauldron**, may antedate Christian times.

The church itself, named after Catan's nephew,
Blane, dates from the 12th century, a two-
compartment building with a relatively well-
preserved chevron-moulded Norman arch in the
high dividing gable. Nearby, in the lower
churchyard, are the foundations of an earlier
chapel doubtless laid waste by the Norsemen,
and, all around, the graves of a millennium of
Christian life and death which continued here
until the 18th century. In such a spot it is easy to
sense both the frailty of man and the love of God.

The road south from Kerrycroy skirts Mount
Stuart estate. **Scoulag Lodge**, 1896-8, by
Robert Weir Schultz can only be called
Baronial vernacular: white roughcast walls,
Arts & Crafts gablets, a conical stair turret and
three emblazoned escutcheons. The plan is
wedge-shaped with rooms cleverly clustered
around a six-flue central chimney stack.

Scoulag Lodge

At **Kingarth Hotel**, a crow-stepped farmhouse
now an inn, a road runs down past the old
school and some decoratively patterned brick
cottages, to the township of Kilchattan Bay.
Strung out along the shore, but for a few
single-storey dwellings almost everything dates
from the 1870s or later, from that period of

holiday boom that brought
people to what had been remote, rather
picturesque backwater.

Some plain two-storey houses with pilastered
doorways are brightened by names such as
Daisybank, **Bloomfield**, **Lilybank** and
Rockvale, 1874. There are several red
sandstone terraces, such as **Beechland**, 1877
and **Hendryfield**, 1879; a few tenements, such
as **Albert Place**, *c.*1885, still with its original
shops; a three-storey hotel, **St Blane's Hotel**,
which has a central lampshade roof tasselled
with timber bracketing along the eaves; and
Kingarth & Kilchattan Bay Church, 1890,
gable-fronted with a stiffly geometrical wheel
window. But of the ancient Celtic cell of St
Catan only an eponymous memory remains –
though the site of his well may be discovered
near **Little Kilchattan Farm** on the northern
side of the bay.

Kilchattan Bay

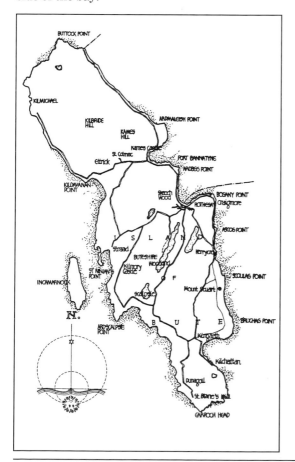

Many people have helped us in the compilation of this book. Charles McKean and David Walker have both read our texts and we are particularly grateful for their suggestions, information and criticisms. Duncan McAra's editorial comments have been most valuable. We also wish to record our thanks to Catherine Cruft; Ian Gow and the staff at the Royal Commission on the Ancient & Historical Monuments of Scotland; to Bernadette Goslin of Historic Scotland; to John Hood at Clydebank Central Library; Michael C Taylor, Graham Hopner and Mary Bannister of Dumbarton District Libraries; Murdo MacDonald, Archivist with Argyll & Bute District Council; William Scott at Dunoon District Library; Anne Buchanan of the Buteshire Natural History Society and Edward Monaghan of Bute Library, Rothesay; to the planning office of Dumbarton District Council; to Alan Berry, S Lothian Barclay, Elaine Campbell, Kirsteen Holmes, Ann Millar, Helen Robertson and Bert Shaw; to AHAUS, the Archive of Historical Architecture at the University of Strathclyde, to the Helensburgh & District Civic Society; and to our indulgent employers, the Department of Architecture & Building Science, University of Strathclyde, and Michael and Sue Thornley, Architects; to all those architects who have readily responded with help and information to our enquiries; and to the many owners of properties who have so hospitably entertained and informed us. Thanks are due to all at the RIAS for achieving publication in the face of many difficulties and setbacks.

Though the guide attempts to be comprehensive, it cannot hope to be all-inclusive. For omissions which may irritate the reader we apologise, as we do for all errors. Special thanks are due to Ellen Thomson and Susan Thomson for patient typing of repeatedly revised manuscripts.

A guide such as this permits only the briefest referencing of sources. We have consulted numerous histories, local records, guidebooks, pamphlets, etc. and can name only the more significant of these.

Agnew, J, **The Story of the Vale of Leven**, 1975; Aiton, W, **General View of the Agriculture of the County of Bute**, 1816; Billings, R W, **The Baronial and Ecclesiastical Antiquities of Scotland**, 1852; Brown, A, **The History of Cowal**, 1908; Bruce, J, **History of the Parish of West or Old Kilpatrick**, 1893; Butt, J, **The Industrial Archaeology of Scotland**, 1967; Ferguson, J & Temple J G, **The Old Vale and Its Memories**, 1927; Fleming, J A, **Helensburgh and the Three Lochs**, 1956; Groome, F H, **Ordnance Gazeteer of Scotland**, 1882-5; Hewison, J K, **The Isle of Bute in the Olden Time**, 1893-5; Hood, J, **The History of Clydebank**, 1988; Hume, J R, **The Industrial Archaeology of Scotland**, 1976; Irving, J, **Dumbartonshire: County and Burgh**, 1920; Jones, A F, **Cardross, the Village in Days Gone By**, 1985; Laing, R M, **Helensburgh and Rhu – The First Hundred Years**, 1973; Leighton, J M, **Strath-Clutha or The Beauties of the Clyde**, no date; MacGibbon, D and Ross, T, **The Castellated and Domestic Architecture of Scotland**, 1887-92, MacLeod, D, **The Clyde District of Dumbartonshire**, 1886; MacPhail, I M M, **A Short History of Dumbartonshire**, 1962; Maughan, W C, **Rosneath Past and Present**, 1893 and **Annals of Garelochside**, 1897; Monteith, J and McCrorie, I, **Clyde Piers – A Pictorial Record**, 1982; Neill, J, **Records and Reminiscences of Bonhill Parish**, 1912; **The Statistical Accounts of Scotland**; Osborne, B D, **Helensburgh and Garelochside in Old Pictures**, 1980; Ure, D, **General View of the Agriculture in the County of Dumbarton**, 1794; Whyte, A and Macfarlan, D, **General View of the Agriculture in the County of Dumbarton**, 1811.

The source of each photograph is credited alongside. Particular thanks, however, are due to Anne Dick and the RCAHMS.

1. Architrave (projecting ornamental frame)
2. Astragal (glazing bar)
3. Barge (gable board)
4. Basement, raised
5. Bullseye, keyblocked (circular window with projecting blocks punctuating frame)
6. Buttress (supporting projection)
7. Caphouse (top chamber)
8. Cartouche (decorative tablet)
9. Cherrycocking (masonry joints filled with small stones)
10. Channelled ashlar (recessed horizontal joints in smooth masonry)
11. Chimneycope, corniced
12. Chimneycope, moulded
13. Close (alley)
14. Cobbles
15. Console (scroll bracket)
16. Corbel (projection support)
17. Crowsteps
18. Cutwater (wedge-shaped end of bridge pier)
19. Doocot, lectern
20. Dormer, canted & piended
21. Dormer, pedimented (qv) wallhead
22. Dormer, piended (see under 'roof')
23. Dormer, swept wallhead
24. Fanlight (glazed panel above door)
25. Finial (crowning ornament)
26. Fly-over stair
27. Forestair, pillared
28. Gable, wallhead
29. Gable, wallhead chimney

30. Gable, Dutch (curved)
31. Gibbs doorway (framed with projecting stonework)
32. Harling
33. Hoist, fishing net
34. Hoodmoulding (projection over opening to divert rainwater)
35. Jettied (overhanging)
36. Lucarne (small dormer on spire)
37. Margin, stone
38. Mercat Cross
39. Marriage Lintel
40. Mullion (vertical division of window)
41. Nave (main body of church)
42. Pavilion (building attached by wing to main building)
43. Pediment (triangular ornamental feature above windows etc)
44. Portico
45. Quoins, rusticated (corner stones with recessed joints)
46. Refuge (recess in bridge parapet)
47. Ridge, crested
48. Roof, flared pyramidal
49. Roof, leanto
50. Roof, ogival (with S-curve pitch generally rising from square plan and meeting at point)
51. Roof, pantiled
52. Roof, piended (formed by intersecting roof slopes)
53. Roof, slated

54. Skew (gable coping)
55. Skewputt, moulded (lowest stone of skew, qv)
56. Skewputt, scroll
57. Stair jamb (projection containing stairway)
58. Stringcourse (horizontal projecting wall moulding)
59. Transept (transverse wing of cruciform church)
60. Transom (horizontal division of window)
61. Voussoir (wedge-shaped stone forming archway)
62. Tympanum (area within pediment qv)
63. Window, bay (projecting full-height from ground level)
64. Window, oriel (corbelled bay qv)
65. Window, sash & case (sliding sashes within case)

INDEX

NORTH CLYDE ESTUARY

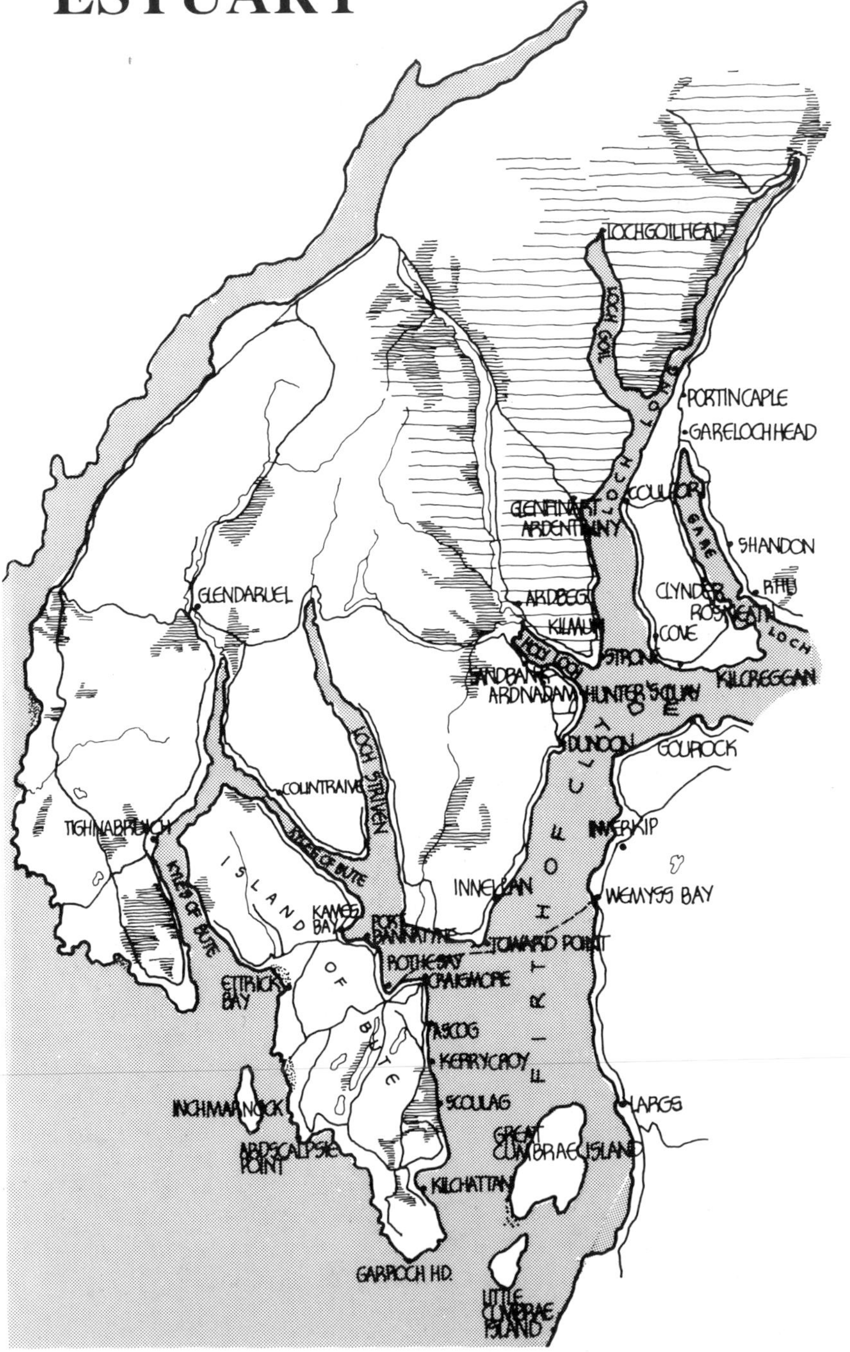

LOCHGOILHEAD
LOCH GOIL
LOCH LONG
PORTINCAPLE
GARELOCHHEAD
COULPORT
GARE
GLENFINART
ARDENTINNY
SHANDON
CLYNDER
ROSNEATH
RHU
LOCH
ARDBEG
KILMUN
HOLY LOCH
COVE
STRONE
KILCREGGAN
SANDBANK
ARDNADAM
HUNTER'S QUAY
DUNOON
GOUROCK
GLENDARUEL
COLINTRAIVE
LOCH STRIVEN
KYLES OF BUTE
TIGHNABRUAICH
INVERKIP
FIRTH OF CLYDE
ISLAND OF BUTE
INNELLAN
WEMYSS BAY
KAMES BAY
PORT BANNATYNE
TOWARD POINT
ROTHESAY
CRAIGMORE
ETTRICK BAY
ASCOG
KERRYCROY
SCOULAG
INCHMARNOCK
LARGS
GREAT CUMBRAE ISLAND
ARDSCALPSIE POINT
KILCHATTAN
GARROCH HD.
LITTLE CUMBRAE ISLAND